Pictures

of

Grace

FRAZER 365

Pictures of Grace

Daily Devotions for Advent

Frazer Discipleship

What is Frazer 365?

Frazer 365 is one church's attempt to touch every member every day with the Word of God. Acts 2:46 teaches that the early church met **"day by day, attending the temple together."** While most members cannot get to our campus every day, we can still study His Word daily together in community. We believe that God works in miraculous ways when every member studies the same Scripture each day. We have also discovered that an expositional approach to the study of Scripture keeps us from skipping the difficult sections and provides us the whole counsel of God's Word.

At Frazer, we believe that the Word of God **"is living and active."** (Hebrews 4:12a)

The Bible is alive with God's truth, and it activates our spiritual growth. Proper application to our daily lives works to help us follow His will.

At Frazer, we believe that the Word of God is **"sharper than any two-edged sword, piercing to the division of soul and of spirit, of joints and of marrow."** (Hebrews 4:12b)

The Bible properly divided, penetrates our lives, and reveals the core of who we are meant to be in Christ. Scripture clearly cuts to the heart of God's purpose and plan for the life He has given us. At times, it painfully points out the sin in our lives.

At Frazer, we believe that the Word of God discerns **"the thoughts and intentions of the heart."** (Hebrews 4:12c)

The Holy Spirit speaks to us through God's Word and uncovers our thoughts and intentions. Scripture points out wrong thinking and misdirected motives and guides us back to a godly mindset, unselfish attitude, and a serving spirit.

At Frazer, we believe that: **"All Scripture is breathed out by God and profitable for teaching, for reproof, for correction, and for training in righteousness, that the man of God may be complete, equipped for every good work."** (2 Timothy 3:16-17)

At Frazer, we believe that His Word is **"a lamp to my feet."** (Psalm 119:105a)

Godly Wisdom comes from His Word. Scripture shines a light on God's will so you can see where He wants your next steps to be.

At Frazer, we believe that His Word is **"a light to my path."** (Psalm 119:105b)

As you commit to **Frazer 365**, may His Word illuminate your path as you take daily steps of faith in your journey with Him.

Pictures of Grace

Matthew 1:1, 3, 5-6, 16

[1] The book of the genealogy of Jesus Christ,
the son of David, the son of Abraham. . .
[3] and Judah the father of Perez and Zerah by **Tamar**, . . .
[5] and Salmon the father of Boaz by **Rahab**,
and Boaz the father of Obed by **Ruth**,
and Obed the father of Jesse,
[6] and Jesse the father of David the king.
And David was the father of Solomon
by **the wife of Uriah**, . . .
[16] and Jacob the father of Joseph the husband of
Mary, of whom Jesus was born,
who is called Christ.

Table of Contents

Pictures of Grace

Introduction

Today, we embark on an Advent journey entitled **Pictures of Grace**. According to the genealogy of Jesus in Matthew 1:1-15, the following five women are included: Tamar, Rahab, Ruth, Bathsheba, and Mary. Each of these ladies are clear pictures and vivid reminders of God's marvelous grace. And last time I checked, there is not a person on the planet (past, present, or future) that doesn't need the unmerited favor of Almighty God. Therefore, this study and these devotionals are for all of us.

But what is grace? We will never be able to be delivered by it if we can't even define it. In other words, if we don't know what grace is, how do we know if we have it? I don't remember where I read this following definition of grace; I just know that it was the great expositor, Warren Wiersbe, who said it. In fact, I will never forget it because he put the definition in the form of an acrostic.

G – God's
R – Riches
A – At
C – Christ's
E – Expense

Grace is "God's riches at Christ's expense." Not only can I remember that, but it just makes biblical sense to me.

Because of what Jesus did for me at the cross and in an empty tomb, I get the riches of God and Christ paid the expense. He purchased my salvation and more by shedding His blood and dying for my sins.

This emphasis on grace is what Paul is sharing with the church at Ephesus. Read the following Scripture and watch carefully for the word grace found two times.

Ephesians 1:3-10

[3] Blessed be the God and Father of our Lord Jesus Christ, who has blessed us in Christ with every spiritual blessing in the heavenly places, [4] even as He chose us in Him before the foundation of the world, that we should be holy and blameless before Him. In love [5] He predestined us for adoption to Himself as sons through Jesus Christ, according to the purpose of His will, [6] to the praise of His glorious grace, with which He has blessed us in the Beloved. [7] In Him we have redemption through His blood, the forgiveness of our trespasses, according to the riches of His grace, [8] which He lavished upon us, in all wisdom and insight [9] making known to us the mystery of His will, according to His purpose, which He set forth in Christ [10] as a plan for the fullness of time, to unite all things in Him, things in heaven and things on earth.

That's a lot of riches at Christ's expense! God's grace has given us "every spiritual blessing in the heavenly places." God did this "to the praise of His glorious grace." And we have redemption and forgiveness "according to the riches of His grace." Hallelujah! Praise His name!

This all reminds me of a song from a long time ago. Elvina M. Hall defined grace back in 1865 when, quite frankly, she got bored in church. She was a 47-year-old church member who had lost her husband. This widow was letting her mind wander after

2

a long prayer by her pastor and an even longer sermon. She was sitting in the choir loft of the Monument Methodist Episcopal Church in Baltimore, Maryland. While she was thinking deeply about God, she opened a hymnal and wrote down a poem on the inside cover. She gave the poem to her pastor at the end of the church service. That little poem would later become the famous hymn—"Jesus Paid it All." Mrs. Hall's words were, "Jesus paid it all; all to Him I owe. Sin had left a crimson stain, He washed it white as snow."

Let's get started and may God overwhelm you during this Advent season with pictures of the riches of His grace!

Pictures of Grace

The Experience of Grace

God's grace is compelling when explained,
but irresistible when experienced.
Kyle Idleman, *Grace is Greater*[1]

Text: Matthew 1:1-3
[1] The book of the genealogy of Jesus Christ, the son of David, the son of Abraham. [2] Abraham was the father of Isaac, and Isaac the father of Jacob, and Jacob the father of Judah and his brothers, [3] and Judah the father of Perez and Zerah by Tamar, and Perez the father of Hezron, and Hezron the father of Ram, . . .

Thoughts:
The Bible is a book with a long list of people who have messed up. In fact, some of the greatest heroes of our faith have some dreadful past sins to deal with. Old Testament Professor and author, David Lamb, stated that "sections of the Old Testament could be renamed 'Humans Behaving Badly' because both godly men (Jacob, Judah, and David) and godly women (Tamar, Rahab, and Ruth) appear to be involved in unholy behavior."

Notice the great insights David Lamb gives to the need for grace:

A reason to examine these stories of messed-up heroes of the faith is that they have powerful lessons to teach us. When we ignore their stories, we deny the power of God's grace, because as humans' bad behavior abounds, God's gracious behavior abounds even more (Romans 5:20). Time and time again we see that when humans behave badly, God behaves graciously.[2]

Now, notice how this author makes the connection to the women of Advent.

> The first woman mentioned in the New Testament isn't Mary the mother of Jesus or Elizabeth the mother of John the Baptist. When you realize that Matthew begins with a genealogy, you might think the first woman of the New Testament would be the first woman of the Old Testament, Eve. Nope. Well, then, surely it has to be one of the wives of the patriarchs, Sarah, Rebekah, or Leah. Nope, nope, nope. The first woman of the New Testament is Tamar (Matt. 1:3).[3]

I thought these segments from Lamb's book would get your attention as we start our study of **Pictures of Grace**. In the days ahead, we will study in detail their stories. Yet, we all need to experience God's grace. Both the Old Testament and New Testament start with great examples of our sin problem. Because we all share this same sin nature, we all need to experience God's grace. Talking about grace is helpful, but only experiencing grace brings healing. I hope that as you journey through these devotions, the Sunday services at our Church, along with the weekly Bible Studies; that God would use all these as tools to lead you to experience His grace.

Questions:

1. How would you define the grace of God?

2. In what ways are you experiencing His grace?

3. How can you demonstrate grace while receiving it?

Day Two

Pictures of Grace

Interrupted by Grace

Men may fall by sin but cannot raise themselves up
without the help of grace.
John Bunyan[1]

Text: Genesis 38:1-5

[1] It happened at that time that Judah went down from his brothers and turned aside to a certain Adullamite, whose name was Hirah. [2] There Judah saw the daughter of a certain Canaanite whose name was Shua. He took her and went in to her, [3] and she conceived and bore a son, and he called his name Er. [4] She conceived again and bore a son, and she called his name Onan. [5] Yet again she bore a son, and she called his name Shelah. Judah was in Chezib when she bore him.

Thoughts:

Today we begin our study of the account of Tamar found in Genesis 38. The first five verses introduce us to Tamar's future father-in-law, Judah, and her future husband, Er. Remember their names as we see how God will bring His Son, our Savior, through Tamar's offspring.

If you were walking through Genesis, this chapter would seem out of place. Most scholars outline Genesis 37-50 as "The story of Joseph and his brothers." So why would God put the strange and sinful story of Tamar as an apparent interruption right after the story of Joseph gets started? Well, it is an interruption and illustration of grace. God's grace! Grace that not only is greater than our sin, but grace that is displayed in the family tree of His Son!

God's Word has so many interruptions of grace. The fact that God calls Himself—"The God of Abraham, Isaac, and Jacob" is a symbol of grace! Abraham is about to sacrifice his son Isaac on the altar. But God interrupts him with a call of grace and a ram as a substitute. When Isaac was old, Jacob tricked him out of blessing the firstborn Esau. Yet God again interrupted with grace and gave Jacob twelve sons. Jacob would be in the lineage of Jesus. In fact, his fourth-born son, Judah, will have physical relations with his daughter-in-law named Tamar. Instead of delivering judgment, God displays His grace and orchestrates it into His plan.

This whole story of Tamar starts with Judah not being with his brothers. Maybe he felt guilty because it was his idea to sell Joseph as a slave. (Genesis 37:26-27). Whatever the case, Judah moves away from his family and marries a Canaanite woman. This was something that Abraham avoided for Isaac (Genesis 24:3) and Isaac avoided for Jacob (Genesis 28:1). Judah followed in the footsteps of his uncles, Ishmael and Esau, who both also married Canaanite women. This was strictly forbidden in Deuteronomy 7:3-4.

One of the greatest temptations faced by the nation of Israel in their Promise Land living was conforming to the worldly nations around them. It doesn't take long to fall into sin if you isolate yourself from your faith family and start socializing with those who idolize the world.

We can learn a lot from Judah and Tamar. Worldly decisions can have huge spiritual implications. We are all just one step away from sliding into sin. Yet, God in His love, keeps intervening with interruptions of grace. Thank You, Jesus, for Your patience, forgiveness, and restoration!

Questions:

1. In what ways has God interrupted your life with His grace?

2. How can you live forgiven without abusing His grace?

3. How does the message of Song of Solomon 2:15 relate to Judah's decisions? *"It's the little foxes that spoil the vine."*

Day Three

Pictures of Grace

The Law of Grace

Grace is love in action.
G. Campbell Morgan[1]

Text: Genesis 38:6-11
⁶ And Judah took a wife for Er his firstborn, and her name was Tamar. ⁷ But Er, Judah's firstborn, was wicked in the sight of the Lord, and the Lord put him to death. ⁸ Then Judah said to Onan, "Go in to your brother's wife and perform the duty of a brother-in-law to her, and raise up offspring for your brother." ⁹ But Onan knew that the offspring would not be his. So whenever he went in to his brother's wife he would waste the semen on the ground, so as not to give offspring to his brother. ¹⁰ And what he did was wicked in the sight of the Lord, and he put him to death also. ¹¹ Then Judah said to Tamar his daughter-in-law, "Remain a widow in your father's house, till Shelah my son grows up"—for he feared that he would die, like his brothers. So Tamar went and remained in her father's house.

Thoughts:
Tamar's husband, Er, dies before she has a child. This leaves her in a whole lot of trouble. A childless widow in biblical days would lose her identity and her inheritance. Her husband had been the firstborn and would have inherited a double portion of Judah's inheritance. Now, without a son as an heir, Er's portion will go to his brothers. Tamar is left with nothing.

God put a law in His Word for the nation of Israel to protect against widows in Tamar's situation. Even in God's laws, we find His mercy and grace. If we are not careful, we will see God's laws as limits and not as liberation. God's laws not only lead us to His grace; they also protect us by His grace. This particular law is found in Deuteronomy 25 in a section of Scripture entitled, "Law's Concerning Levirate Marriage." The expression "levirate marriage" comes from the Latin, *levir*, for "brother-in-law."[2] Here is the law in Deuteronomy 25:5-6:

> [5] If brothers dwell together, and one of them dies and has no son, the wife of the dead man shall not be married outside the family to a stranger. Her husband's brother shall go in to her and take her as his wife and perform the duty of a husband's brother to her. [6] And the first son whom she bears shall succeed to the name of his dead brother, that his name may not be blotted out of Israel.

Judah does the right thing according to the law, but with a questionable motive. He sends his next-oldest son, Onan, with the declaration, "Go… perform the duty of a brother-in-law, and raise up offspring for your brother." As you read the account in Genesis 38, you get the idea that Onan responds out of duty and not out of love for his family.

Tom Fuerst gives a clear picture of what Onan was struggling with in obeying the Levirate Law.

> This obligation to provide children for her and his deceased brother provides a greater headache for him than for his father. By taking on this responsibility, Onan puts his (and his sons') own inheritance at

risk. As the oldest son, Er had the right to a double portion of his father's estate upon Judah's death. That larger share would have passed to Onan after Er's death, but the Levirate Law now called that into question. Presumably, the children Onan provided for Er would receive Er's inheritance. To do the right thing, Onan must forfeit his potential personal gain. Tamar represents a financial liability, a threat to his inheritance.[3]

Onan goes through with the physical act of sleeping with Tamar but makes sure that she cannot conceive a child. He takes part in his own pleasure but will not do what it takes to ease Tamar's pain. His selfishness keeps him from doing what is legal, ethical, and God's will to protect the widows of that day. Onan is a picture of the world. Onan tried to obey the law partially and please God fully. He wanted to save face more than he wanted to serve faithfully.

The law given in Deuteronomy 25 goes on to describe what should happen if a brother-in-law fails to fulfill his responsibility. It is found in Deuteronomy 25:7-10:

> [7] And if the man does not wish to take his brother's wife, then his brother's wife shall go up to the gate to the elders and say, 'My husband's brother refuses to perpetuate his brother's name in Israel; he will not perform the duty of a husband's brother to me.' [8] Then the elders of his city shall call him and speak to him, and if he persists, saying, 'I do not wish to take her,' [9] then his brother's wife shall go up to him in the presence of the elders and pull his sandal off his foot and spit in his face. And she shall answer and say, 'So shall it be done to the man who does not build up his

brother's house.' ¹⁰ And the name of his house shall be called in Israel, 'The house of him who had his sandal pulled off.'

Onan did not want to have a bad reputation, so he appeared to fulfill the Levirate Law. He should have had his face spit on, and labeled, "The house of him who had his sandal pulled off."

I have wondered why God gave the punishment of taking off his sandal in public. Could this possibly be where we get the phrase "walking in someone else's shoes"? Maybe. That is just my crazy way of thinking. However, it does give a whole new meaning to "the shoes on the other foot"!

Tremper Longman III, in his commentary, makes a connection with this law and another woman of advent: Ruth.

> The closest we see this scenario work out is in Ruth 4, when Boaz approaches a relative who is closer to Naomi than he is about marrying Ruth. Onan makes no public protest, but privately refuses to follow through on his duty. Since he does not protest publicly, Tamar would not have the option, if it was even available to her in this environment which is earlier and non-Israelite, to challenge his refusal. God, however, knows what Onan does in private, and for his evil actions, God put him to death.⁴

Whatever the case, Onan wouldn't extend grace, so God sent His judgment. Therein lies great lessons for us. Grace extended is grace received and God loves you so much that grace is seen even in His laws.

Questions:

1. How are you tempted to save face rather than extend grace?

2. How does today's devotion relate to what Jesus said in Matthew 5:7? *"Blessed are the merciful, for they shall receive mercy."*

3. What are your thoughts on the law of the sandal?

Day Four

Pictures of Grace

The Cost of Grace

Grace is free only because the
giver Himself has borne the cost.
Phillip Yancey, *What's so Amazing about Grace?*[1]

Text: Genesis 38:12-19

[12] In the course of time the wife of Judah, Shua's daughter, died. When Judah was comforted, he went up to Timnah to his sheepshearers, he and his friend Hirah the Adullamite.

[13] And when Tamar was told, "Your father-in-law is going up to Timnah to shear his sheep," [14] she took off her widow's garments and covered herself with a veil, wrapping herself up, and sat at the entrance to Enaim, which is on the road to Timnah. For she saw that Shelah was grown up, and she had not been given to him in marriage. [15] When Judah saw her, he thought she was a prostitute, for she had covered her face.

[16] He turned to her at the roadside and said, "Come, let me come in to you," for he did not know that she was his daughter-in-law. She said, "What will you give me, that you may come in to me?" [17] He answered, "I will send you a young goat from the flock." And she said, "If you give me a pledge, until you send it—" [18] He said, "What pledge shall I give you?" She replied, "Your signet and your cord and your staff that is in your hand." So he gave them to her and went in to her, and she conceived by him. [19] Then she arose and went away, and taking off her veil she put on the garments of her widowhood.

Thoughts:

Tamar was in a tough spot in her journey of life. She needed to come up with a plan. Her plan was only as good as Judah's immorality. It would not work if Judah didn't give in to the temptation. Something about Judah's past gave Tamar the idea for her future.

Sin has a way of blindsiding us. Temptation can come out of nowhere, which is why we must always be spiritually prepared. One commentary described Judah's scenario this way:

> That this was an unplanned stop on his trip is proven by the fact that Judah had nothing to pay for her services. She requested compensation. He offered to send her a young goat from his flock later. Tamar wanted something as a pledge that he would keep his promise. He wanted to know what she desired. She requested his signet **seal** (the instrument he used to sign his name on clay) and his **staff** (38:18). He complied.[2]

Judah's sin would cost, and he didn't have a way to pay for it. Isn't that always the case with sin? Sin always cost and the cost of grace is beyond what any of us can afford. Sin is also personal as is evidenced in what Tamar requested for a down payment for his sin. These items are intriguing.

These are identity markers. A seal was used on soft clay to leave an impression that was unique to Judah. The walking stick would also have features that would connect it to Judah. Leaving these items would be like leaving a driver's license or a credit card today.[3]

Sin is both personal and costly. And Jesus personally paid the price for the grace He offers with His sacrificial death.

Questions:

1. How does the cost of grace increase the value of grace?

2. How do the personal belongings of Judah relate to the personal impact of sin?

3. How can your life be a daily "Thank-You" to God?

Pictures of Grace

Grace Delayed

*Our ability to appreciate grace is in direct correlation
to the degree to which we acknowledge our need for it.
The more I recognize the ugliness of my sin,
the more I can appreciate the beauty of God's grace.*
Kyle Idleman, *Grace is Greater*[1]

Text: Genesis 38:20-23

[20] When Judah sent the young goat by his friend the Adullamite to take back the pledge from the woman's hand, he did not find her. [21] And he asked the men of the place, "Where is the cult prostitute who was at Enaim at the roadside?" And they said, "No cult prostitute has been here."

[22] So he returned to Judah and said, "I have not found her. Also, the men of the place said, 'No cult prostitute has been here.'" [23] And Judah replied, "Let her keep the things as her own, or we shall be laughed at. You see, I sent this young goat, and you did not find her."

Thoughts:

Judah is caught between his sin and the consequences. He is having a hard time hiding his shame. In more ways than one, his true identity is at stake. He knows that he has sinned. He also knows that the other woman has concrete proof of his identity. Therefore, Judah goes from the commission of sin to the attempted covering of sin.

19

Judah sends payment of the goat with his friend to find the woman. His main objective is to get his stuff back so that he can keep his sin from going public.

The language of the Old Testament is very interesting here. When Judah's friend asked people if they have seen the prostitute, he uses a unique term. The ESV translates it as "cult prostitute," but the word in the Hebrew here simply means "holy woman." Genesis 38:15 states that Judah thought Tamar was a "prostitute." Now, Judah's friend is asking people for a "holy woman." It appears that Judah's friend is trying extremely hard to preserve Judah's reputation.

When Tamar cannot be found, Judah responds, "Let her keep the things as her own, or we shall be laughed at." Several spiritual truths stem from Judah's statement.

First of all, you can never conceal your sin. The fact that Tamar still had proof of Judah's sin must have kept him awake at night. Imagine the worry of knowing that at any moment, the world could discover your secret sin. However, if you could get all the proof of your mistakes back, God still knows!

Second, Judah didn't want to become a laughingstock. He didn't want to look like a fool, or for the joke to be on him. If he kept looking for a prostitute so he could get back his belongings, more people would find out that he slept with a prostitute. Anytime you or I fall into sin and take Satan's bait, the joke is on us. Every time we give in to temptation, we play the fool. God's will is too important and sin's consequences too severe to let our spiritual guards down. When we admit our sin, God is faithful to extend His grace. Why wait to receive His favor?

Questions:

1. Have you ever been caught between your sin and the impending consequences? Explain how.

2. How can the last phrase of Numbers 32:23 help your decision to come clean before God? *". . . and be sure your sin will find you out."*

3. How does running from your sin escalate bad decisions?

4. Spend some moments meditating on the implications of James 5:16. *"Therefore, confess your sins to one another and pray for one another, that you may be healed. The prayer of a righteous person has great power as it is working."*

Day Six

Pictures of Grace

A Perspective of Grace

Grace often grows strongest.
where conviction of sin has pierced deepest.
Sinclair Ferguson[1]

Text: Genesis 38:24-26

[24] About three months later Judah was told, "Tamar your daughter-in-law has been immoral. Moreover, she is pregnant by immorality." And Judah said, "Bring her out, and let her be burned." [25] As she was being brought out, she sent word to her father-in-law, "By the man to whom these belong, I am pregnant." And she said, "Please identify whose these are, the signet and the cord and the staff." [26] Then Judah identified them and said, "She is more righteous than I, since I did not give her to my son Shelah." And he did not know her again.

Thoughts:

It is much easier to judge the sins of others instead of looking at your own personal sins. It is also easier to see in others what you refuse to see in yourself. This characteristic of our fallen nature will be displayed throughout our study. (We will see it again in David's response to Nathan's story when we discuss Bathsheba). But for now, we need to recognize the tendency we all have to be judgmental. If not regularly checked, we could desire that others be punished for the same sins we ask God to forgive us for.

As soon as Judah discovered that Tamar had gotten pregnant, he responded with judgment. Kent Hughes describes Judah's response with this statement, "Judah's violent declaration suggests that he may have jumped at the opportunity to have her out of the way once and for all."[2] Judah was as quick to condemn Tamar as he was to cover his own sin! But he will soon discover that the signs of his sins are everywhere.

Tamar has his belongings, which quickly puts everything into the proper perspective for Judah. As my grandfather used to say, "Be careful when you point your finger at someone, because when you point one finger at others, you always have three more fingers pointing back at you."

God has a way of reminding us of our need for Him. Judah and Tamar both had to deal personally with their own sins. Judah needed the same grace that Tamar needed.

The chapter thus presents a predominantly negative portrait of Judah. He lives among and befriends Canaanites. He does not do the right thing by his widowed daughter-in-law. He sleeps with a prostitute, and callously orders the death of his daughter-in-law with no further inquiry. However, Judah is not totally depraved. When confronted, he is able to recognize his guilt. Perhaps here we see the beginning of Judah's turnaround. Indeed, as the Joseph narrative continues, Judah is back with his brothers and the assumption is that he is no longer living among the Canaanites.[3]

We all need God's grace. None of us are righteous outside Jesus Christ. We need to keep a perspective of grace.

Questions:

1. When it comes to sin, do you find yourself being more judgmental of others and more gracious toward yourself? Explain your response.

2. How can you keep a biblical perspective of grace so that you won't be controlled by a critical and judgmental nature?

3. What are your thoughts on the following statement from today's devotion? "Judah needed the same grace that Tamar needed."

Day Seven

Pictures of Grace

Grace Displayed

God's grace is not only amazing grace,
but also abounding grace.
Vance Havner[1]

Text: Genesis 38:27-30

[27] When the time of her labor came, there were twins in her womb. [28] And when she was in labor, one put out a hand, and the midwife took and tied a scarlet thread on his hand, saying, "This one came out first." [29] But as he drew back his hand, behold, his brother came out. And she said, "What a breach you have made for yourself!" Therefore his name was called Perez. [30] Afterward his brother came out with the scarlet thread on his hand, and his name was called Zerah.

Thoughts:

I love the way God displays His grace. He truly is "able to do far more abundantly than all that we ask or think, according to the power at work within us." (Ephesians 3:20). God takes a wicked situation and brings a double blessing from it. Twins! Only God would bring two new lives out of two sinful ones. His grace abounds in unbelievable ways!

The symbolism in the birth of the twins is amazing. One commentary explained it as follows:

The chapter ends with an account of the birth of the twin boys born to Judah and to Tamar. The unusual nature of the birth indicates a struggle for primacy and explains the names given to the children. While one of the children stuck his hand out of the womb and was declared the "first," having a scarlet thread tied to his wrist, he soon drew the hand back into the womb. Thus, unexpectedly, the other child actually emerged first, receiving the name Perez or "breaking out." Then the child with the scarlet thread was born, receiving the name Zerah, which means "brilliance" or perhaps "scarlet."[2]

A crimson thread and a baby "breaking out." There is a crimson thread of God's grace that runs from Genesis to Revelation. His grace is always on display. His grace is breaking out in lives every single day.

It is intriguing to me that Jesus would later descend from Perez' side of the family. Jesus wouldn't come through the line of Zerah, which means scarlet thread. Salvation will not be through man's effort to tie a red ribbon on a potential firstborn. Salvation will come through the breaking out of God's grace on a world that desperately needs Him.

Grace is displayed all over Genesis 38. There is grace for Tamar, her twins, and Judah. There is grace for all of us knowing that Jesus comes through a family tree of messed-up sinners to bring us all salvation.

As great as Judah's sins were, it is evident that God also worked in the situation for good, since from this incest came Perez, one of the ancestors of the Lord Jesus Christ. Is it not strange that Christ should trace His ancestry through this illicit son of Judah rather than through Joseph, who is so much like Christ and is so dominant in the final portions of the Book of Genesis?[3]

Questions:

1. How can you focus more on God's grace on display?

2. What are your thoughts on the fact that Jesus comes from Perez's side of the family and not Zerah's?

3. In what specific ways has God poured out His abounding grace on your life? List several ways in the space below and spend some time today thanking Him for His grace.

Pictures of Grace

A Genealogy of Grace

Grace is the undeserved, unmerited,
and loving action of God in human existence
through the ever-present Holy Spirit.
John Wesley, *The Book of Discipline*[1]

Text: Matthew 1:1, 5
[1] The book of the genealogy of Jesus Christ, the son of David, the son of Abraham. . . [5] and Salmon the father of Boaz by Rahab, and Boaz the father of Obed by Ruth, and Obed the father of Jesse,...

Thoughts:

Today, there are a lot of people checking out their family trees to see who hangs in the branches! Businesses that track ancestry are flourishing and there is a renewed interest in family. Genealogies can be intriguing, but none more than the family tree of the one who dates back before creation—Jesus Christ! Matthew's account of Jesus' family tree is a genealogy of grace.

Here is how Bruce Barton describes the beginning of the genealogy in his commentary on Matthew:

Genealogies served several purposes in Bible times. They traced ancestral claims to land and positions of authority, they were outlines for tracing history, and they revealed ancestral origins. Because a person's family line proved his or her standing as one of God's chosen people, Matthew began by showing that Jesus was a descendant of Abraham, the father of all Jews, and a direct descendant of David, fulfilling Old Testament prophecies about the Messiah's line.[2]

But shortly into Jesus' family tree, it gets down-right embarrassing. You would expect the genealogy of God's Son to avoid mentioning anyone with questionable character. But in verse 3, we had Tamar and now in verse 5, we are introduced to Rahab and Ruth. Later in verse 6, we will read "the wife of Uriah" which we all know to be Bathsheba. These four ladies are pictures of God's amazing grace!

For the next several days, we will look at the grace of God that rescues Rahab. For today, we simply want to focus on God's grace that her name is even mentioned in the record. Doing so helps us to be thankful that we can have our names written in His book too—The Lamb's Book of Life. Talk about another book that is a genealogy of grace!!

Biblical scholar, Warren Wiersbe, noted the following about Rahab's name being found in Matthew 1.

> When you read the genealogy of the Lord Jesus Christ in Matthew 1, you find Rahab's name listed there, along with Jacob, David, and the other famous people in the messianic line. She has certainly come a long way from being a pagan prostitute to being an ancestress of the Messiah! "But where sin abounded, grace did much more abound." (Romans 5:20). [3]

We have a lot to be thankful for today. Here is a short list: that Jesus died for our sins, that God would allow us to be called His children, that He would demonstrate His love for us while we were sinners, and for His grace!

Questions:

1. What are your thoughts on Jesus' genealogy of grace?

2. Break down John Wesley's definition of grace in the quote for today. What does each of Wesley's characteristics of God's grace mean to you today?

3. Contemplate God's grace over your life today. Spend some time and add to the short list given today of all you have to be thankful for.

Day Nine

Pictures of Grace

A Closeup Look at Grace

When He says we're forgiven, let's unload the guilt.
When He says we're valuable, let's believe Him. . .
When He says we're provided for, let's stop worrying.
God's efforts are strongest when our efforts are useless.
Max Lucado, *Grace for the Moment*[1]

Text: Joshua 2:1-7

[1] And Joshua the son of Nun sent two men secretly from Shittim as spies, saying, "Go, view the land, especially Jericho." And they went and came into the house of a prostitute whose name was Rahab and lodged there. [2] And it was told to the king of Jericho, "Behold, men of Israel have come here tonight to search out the land." [3] Then the king of Jericho sent to Rahab, saying, "Bring out the men who have come to you, who entered your house, for they have come to search out all the land." [4] But the woman had taken the two men and hidden them. And she said, "True, the men came to me, but I did not know where they were from. [5] And when the gate was about to be closed at dark, the men went out. I do not know where the men went. Pursue them quickly, for you will overtake them." [6] But she had brought them up to the roof and hid them with the stalks of flax that she had laid in order on the roof. [7] So the men pursued after them on the way to the Jordan as far as the fords. And the gate was shut as soon as the pursuers had gone out.

Thoughts:

The story of Rahab begins in Joshua 2. The focus of the book of Joshua before and after this chapter will be on God's deliverance through great conquest. Yet, the narrative of all that God is doing in victory seems to pause for just a moment and give us a closeup look at His amazing grace.

This was highlighted with great insight in the book, *Expecting Emmanuel*:

> That's odd, don't you think? That Israel's top spies are just "men," and the ruler of the entire nation is "the king," while the prostitute alone gets a name? This isn't usually how the biblical text works. Scripture is littered with unnamed women, but this particular woman, Rahab, is named—here in this narrative, in two of the New Testament epistles, and in the genealogy of Jesus.[2]

Even Rahab's introduction in Joshua 2 reveals to us God's unmerited favor.

Rahab was the first Canaanite convert to a belief in Israel's God.[3] The Canaanites are notoriously God's enemy throughout Scripture. Yet, God will rescue Rahab.

One question that arises in this text is, "Why did the spies go to the house of a prostitute? The New American Commentary on Joshua clears up some of the confusion.

> Rahab's house was likely a way station, inn, tavern, or a combination of these. It would have been a logical place for spies to frequent, as a public gathering place and a potential source of information, but it is not necessary to suggest that the spies themselves had (or intended to have) a physical encounter with Rahab.[4]

In our society, people always want to point a finger and judge the sins of others. However, God works through the lives of sinners to bring about His plan of salvation. Only God's grace could reach down and save us. And only God's grace would include people like Rahab to make it happen! Rahab was God's plan for saving the spies. What must the spies have thought when they realized that God had sent a Canaanite woman prostitute to save their lives?![5]

When you look closely at the story of Rahab, you can't help but see your own story there also. Although Rahab is a Canaanite and a prostitute, her deliverance shows that God's grace extends to any person who confesses Him.[6] The fact that Rahab is a prostitute emphasized that a new life can dawn under Yahweh's care even for someone for whom one might not naturally expect such things.[7] No matter how great our past sin, God offers grace and forgiveness.

If you and I would stop today and take a closeup, personal look at our own lives, we would also see pictures of His grace! In John's Gospel, the beloved disciple writes, "For from His fullness we have all received, grace upon grace." John 1:16 (ESV). Notice the progression of this great verse on grace. "For from His fullness" depicts God's grace coming from the totality of all that God is. From His nature, character, integrity, and righteousness, flows His grace. "We have all received" displays the all-inclusive scope of His grace. God's grace doesn't flow just to the top-tier Christian, it is poured out on the lowest of sinners. I praise God today that His grace flows to "whosoever." John 1:16 concludes with this awesome phrase, "grace upon grace." In my past, I have witnessed His grace upon grace. Just as His mercies are new every morning, His grace is available for every mistake. God's grace flows in wave after wave of His ocean full of unmerited favor!

The grace upon grace that God has for your past, is available for your present, and will be forever in your future! The vast resource of His grace does not cause me to downplay the seriousness of sin. It causes me to upgrade my view of God. I never want to abuse His grace, but I am confident that nothing in this life can separate me from His love.

Teach the Text Commentary on Joshua gives a great application story. It is entitled: *"Amazing grace! God can use even you!"* It references *Amazing Grace*, by John Newton.

Newton drew the lyrics of this hymn from the experiences in his own life. Walking away from the faith of his Christian mother, Newton took to the seas and eventually joined a slave-trading ship. In his own words Newton lived a life of moral abandon: "I not only sinned with a high hand myself but made it my study to tempt and seduce others upon every occasion." But the Lord captured his attention on a journey in which his ship was struck by a life-threatening storm. After giving his life to Jesus during that storm, he later became a pastor and the author of numerous hymns. As we see in the story of Rahab, God can use anyone, regardless of his or her past. Will you trust in His amazing grace and allow Him to use you?[8]

Questions:

1. Do a personal closeup inventory of your life today. In what ways is Rahab's story similar to yours?

2. What part of the great hymn *Amazing Grace* is your favorite? Why?

3. How can you rest in His grace as you live for His glory?

Day Ten

Pictures of Grace

The Evidence of Faith

God loves people because of who God is,
not because of who we are.
Phillip Yancey, *What's so Amazing about Grace?*[1]

Text: Joshua 2:8-14

[8] Before the men lay down, she came up to them on the roof [9] and said to the men, "I know that the Lord has given you the land, and that the fear of you has fallen upon us, and that all the inhabitants of the land melt away before you. [10] For we have heard how the Lord dried up the water of the Red Sea before you when you came out of Egypt, and what you did to the two kings of the Amorites who were beyond the Jordan, to Sihon and Og, whom you devoted to destruction. [11] And as soon as we heard it, our hearts melted, and there was no spirit left in any man because of you, for the Lord your God, he is God in the heavens above and on the earth beneath. [12] Now then, please swear to me by the Lord that, as I have dealt kindly with you, you also will deal kindly with my father's house, and give me a sure sign [13] that you will save alive my father and mother, my brothers and sisters, and all who belong to them, and deliver our lives from death." [14] And the men said to her, "Our life for yours even to death! If you do not tell this business of ours, then when the Lord gives us the land we will deal kindly and faithfully with you."

Thoughts:

Rahab's statements in these verses display her growing and genuine faith in God. Note what two scholars have said about her declarations from this portion of God's Word:

> Rahab showed more faith in the Lord than the ten spies had exhibited forty years before, when she said, "I know that the Lord has given you the land" (Joshua 2:9, NKJV). Her faith was based on facts, not just feelings; for she had heard of the miracles God had performed, starting with the opening up of the Red Sea at the Exodus. "So then faith comes by hearing, and hearing by the Word of God" (Romans 10:17, NKJV).[2]

> **The LORD your God is God in heaven above and on the earth below.** This is an amazing statement of faith from a woman who had never tasted manna, had never seen the glory cloud, and had never read the law. Rahab's words become even more significant when we realize that the last part of her affirmation—the phrase 'in the heavens above and the earth below'—is found only three times prior to this, all in contexts that affirm God's exclusive claims to sovereignty. Those texts are Exodus 20:4; Deuteronomy 4:39, and Deuteronomy 5:8.[3]

A long time ago God put this statement on my heart. "However big you think God is, He is bigger than that!" Rahab's faith is growing as her view of God is expanding.

I pray that our faith is doing the same!

Questions:

1. Read Isaiah 40:12-31. You will find a series of questions in this Scripture. Answer them honestly and ask God to give you a glimpse of how enormous He is.

2. What are your thoughts on the following statement from today's devotion? "Rahab showed more faith in the Lord than the ten spies had exhibited forty years before."

3. How is your growing view of God evidenced in your journey of faith?

Day Eleven

Pictures of Grace

The Hope of Grace

Were it not for the grace of God,
there would be no such thing as a Christian.
D. Martyn Lloyd-Jones[1]

Text: Joshua 2:15-21

[15] Then she let them down by a rope through the window, for her house was built into the city wall, so that she lived in the wall. [16] And she said to them, "Go into the hills, or the pursuers will encounter you, and hide there three days until the pursuers have returned. Then afterward you may go your way." [17] The men said to her, "We will be guiltless with respect to this oath of yours that you have made us swear. [18] Behold, when we come into the land, you shall tie this scarlet cord in the window through which you let us down, and you shall gather into your house your father and mother, your brothers, and all your father's household. [19] Then if anyone goes out of the doors of your house into the street, his blood shall be on his own head, and we shall be guiltless. But if a hand is laid on anyone who is with you in the house, his blood shall be on our head. [20] But if you tell this business of ours, then we shall be guiltless with respect to your oath that you have made us swear." [21] And she said, "According to your words, so be it." Then she sent them away, and they departed. And she tied the scarlet cord in the window.

Thoughts:

I ran across a picture on social media that attributed the following quote to D.L. Moody: "There is a scarlet thread running all through the Bible—the whole book points to Christ." Indeed, God's Word was not only written in red, but it was also stained with His blood!

Earlier in our study of Tamar, we saw a red ribbon tied around one of her twins in the womb. Today we find a scarlet cord mentioned in the story of Rahab. The details of Scripture point to a deliverer and Savior.

One commentary points out an intriguing fact about the Hebrew word for "cord" found in these verses:

> Indeed, here the word "cord" (*tiqwah*) may play on the same-sounding word "hope" (*tiqwah*), as if—besides guiding Israel to her house—the dangling rope symbolizes Rahab's expectant hope of survival.[2]

This cord was Rahab's hope. It was her lifeline. If she had this cord hanging out her window, she would be rescued. Likewise, a relationship with Jesus is our cord of hope. When we breathe our last breath on earth, our only hope is Christ in us.

Another commentary emphasizes the red color of this cord of hope.

> The thread's color has attracted attention by students of the Bible, many of whom have argued that its color—the color of blood—is significant, since only through shed blood can redemption come to anyone, whether it be the blood of sacrificial animals in the Old Testament or the blood of Christ in the New Testament (of which the animals' blood was merely an anticipation). This interpretation is very ancient, going back to the Church Fathers.[3]

Questions:

1. What are your thoughts on the quote by D. Martyn Lloyd Jones that begins today's devotion?

2. How is your hope tied to His grace?

3. How is the symbol of the blood of Jesus apparent in your life today as your hope?

Day Twelve

Pictures of Grace

Waiting for Grace

The will of God can never lead you
where the grace of God cannot keep you.
Unknown

You cannot resist the will of God
and receive the grace of God at the same time.
Unknown

Faith is more than thinking something is true. Faith is thinking
something is true to the extent that we act on it.
W. T. Purkiser[1]

Text: Joshua 2:22-24
[22] They departed and went into the hills and remained
there three days until the pursuers returned, and the pursuers
searched all along the way and found nothing. [23] Then the two
men returned. They came down from the hills and passed
over and came to Joshua the son of Nun, and they told him
all that had happened to them. [24] And they said to Joshua,
"Truly the Lord has given all the land into our hands. And also,
all the inhabitants of the land melt away because of us."

Thoughts:
The plan is in place and now Rahab must be patient and
obedient. Waiting is difficult for any follower of Christ. Add
to this waiting, the fear of destruction, and it is a recipe for

complete dependence upon God. What do you do while you are waiting? Well, for Rahab, she keeps the scarlet cord clearly in sight and her faith in God strong in the midst of the fight.

In his commentary on Joshua, Richard Hess gives a great comparison between Joshua and Rahab.

> In the story of Rahab (Chapter 2), Joshua plays no role. It could easily have been omitted, along with its later reference in 6:22—25, and the main plot of the book would not have been affected. However, the story moves the focus from Joshua to Rahab. If Joshua represents the Israelite male who finds guidance and success through faith in the LORD God, does Rahab represent his counterpart, the Canaanite female who also finds guidance and success through faith in the LORD God? In one of the most nationalistic books in the Hebrew Bible, does it not serve the purposes of the promise to Abraham that 'all peoples on earth will be blessed through you' (Genesis 12:3) to place side by side with the choice of a military leader and his initial preparations for battle, the story of a foreign woman who believed and was saved without arms or bloodshed?[2]

Only our God could set Joshua next to Rahab and make them both pictures of grace! Both of them had to grow in their faith through waiting times. Joshua had to wait years for his time to lead. Rahab had to wait days for her city to be destroyed.

But don't get confused and define waiting for grace as a passive break in your life. Neither Joshua nor Rahab pushed pause on their growing faith while they waited. In fact, read Dale Ralph Davis' enlightening words on this matter:

> Here is the evidence of faith. Genuine faith never rests content with being convinced of the reality of God but

presses on to take refuge in God. Rahab not only must know the clear truth about God but also must escape the coming wrath of God. It isn't just a matter of correct belief but of desperate need. Saving faith is always like this. It never stops with brooding over the nature or activity of God but always runs to take refuge under His wings. Amazingly, Rahab not only trembles before the terror of the Lord but also senses that there might be mercy in this fearful God. What but the touch of Yahweh's hand could have created such faith in the heart of this pagan harlot?[3]

As Rahab waits for another display of God's grace, she takes refuge in Him.

If you looked up the definition of refuge, here is what you would find: "A condition of being safe and sheltered from pursuit, danger, or trouble." That is the whole point of finding refuge in God. As you wait for deliverance, you actively pursue finding strength in His presence.

Take some time today and meditate on the following verses found in Scripture about God as your refuge.

Psalm 5:11
But let all who take refuge in You rejoice; let them ever sing for joy, and spread Your protection over them, that those who love Your name may exult in You.

Psalm 16:1
Preserve me, O God, for in You I take refuge.

Psalm 32:7
You are a hiding place for me; You preserve me from trouble; You surround me with shouts of deliverance.

Psalm 36:7

How precious is Your steadfast love, O God! The children of mankind take refuge in the shadow of Your wings.

Psalm 62:8

Trust in Him at all times, O people; pour out your heart before Him; God is a refuge for us.

Psalm 73:28

But for me it is good to be near God; I have made the Lord God my refuge, that I may tell of all Your works.

Psalm 91:1-2

[1] He who dwells in the shelter of the Most High will abide in the shadow of the Almighty. [2] I will say to the Lord, "My refuge and my fortress, my God, in whom I trust."

Just a quick journey through the Psalms will reveal your need to take refuge in Him. As you are waiting patiently for His grace, work passionately at finding refuge in Him.

Questions:

1. If your life was written in chapters like Scripture, what chapter are you in spiritually? Explain your answer.

2. Are you currently waiting for His grace? If so, how are you waiting?

3. In what specific and tangible ways can you take refuge in Him?

4. What are your thoughts about the following quote?

> For the Christian, Rahab's faith provides a model of one who believes in God's historic acts of redemption (whether the exodus of the Old Testament or the cross of the New Testament). Not only does she believe, but she confirms her faith and then acts upon it to preserve God's people and to advance God's kingdom.
> **Richard S. Hess**[4]

Day Thirteen

Pictures of Grace

Rescued by Grace

Grace is stronger than circumstances.
J. C. Ryle[1]

Text: Joshua 6:15-17

[15] On the seventh day they rose early, at the dawn of day, and marched around the city in the same manner seven times. It was only on that day that they marched around the city seven times. [16] And at the seventh time, when the priests had blown the trumpets, Joshua said to the people, "Shout, for the Lord has given you the city. [17] And the city and all that is within it shall be devoted to the Lord for destruction. Only Rahab the prostitute and all who are with her in her house shall live, because she hid the messengers whom we sent."

Thoughts:

In Joshua 6, the walls of Jericho come tumbling down. Whereas Joshua 2 introduces Rahab's story of a red cord, Joshua 6 informs us of God's saving rescue.

On the seventh day of marching around Jericho, the nation of Israel marched around the city seven times. A symbol of completion upon completion. Reminds me of grace upon grace! The priests blow the trumpets, and the people shout. And the walls come tumbling down! God can tear down any wall in your life that is holding you back. He has more than enough grace and power to rescue His people!

After the vocal cords were strained through trumpets and shouts, the red cord was still hanging in the window. You can add to this story the phrase "miracle upon miracles." There are multiple miracles happening here. An entire city collapsing at the sounds of trumpets and shouts is a miracle. Rahab's house is still intact when the walls of Jericho came crashing down is another miracle. That the red cord is visible amid all the devastation is yet another miracle. Our God is a multiple miracle-working God.

Joshua 6 continues the story of rescue in verses 22-25.

> [22] But to the two men who had spied out the land, Joshua said, "Go into the prostitute's house and bring out from there the woman and all who belong to her, as you swore to her." [23] So the young men who had been spies went in and brought out Rahab and her father and mother and brothers and all who belonged to her. And they brought all her relatives and put them outside the camp of Israel. [24] And they burned the city with fire, and everything in it. Only the silver and gold, and the vessels of bronze and of iron, they put into the treasury of the house of the Lord. [25] But Rahab the prostitute and her father's household and all who belonged to her, Joshua saved alive. And she has lived in Israel to this day, because she hid the messengers whom Joshua sent to spy out Jericho.

Our God rescues and our God saves!

Francis Schaeffer asks whether it is "fitting" that God should save such a person, and he answers quite correctly that "it is most fitting." Rahab was no worse than we are, and yet God saves us. It is not the righteous but sinners whom Christ redeems.[2]

Questions:

1. In what specific ways do you view your salvation as a rescue?

2. In what ways have you seen miracles upon miracles in your life?

3. How is God completing His work through you with His miracle working power? If He is not, why not?

Day Fourteen

Pictures of Grace

Grace Transforms

Every day we are objects of the grace of God.
Donald Grey Barnhouse[1]

The worst thing that could happen is that you spend your life trying to outrun God because you think He's chasing you to collect what you owe—when He's really chasing you to give you what you could never afford.
Kyle Idleman, *Grace is Greater* [2]

Text: Hebrews 11:31
[31] By faith Rahab the prostitute did not perish with those who were disobedient, because she had given a friendly welcome to the spies.

Thoughts:
Hebrews 11 is known as the Hall of Fame of Faith. Just note the long list of people that God inducted: Enoch, Abraham, Sarah, Isaac, Jacob, Joseph, Moses, Gideon, David—and the list goes on. But you would expect to find those names there. Notice who else makes the list: Samson and Rahab. Samson failed God and broke all three of his Nazarite vows. God set him apart, but Samson set out to do his own thing. Rahab was a Canaanite prostitute who found God through the destruction of her city. They both finished strong for God.

I believe that God's criteria and the world's criteria for the Hall of Fame of Faith are completely different from one another. While the world looks at fame, God looks at faith.

50

While the world puts significance on gold, God puts His value on people through grace. The world puts all its stock on what is first, God rewards His children for how they finish.

Gene Getz brings up a fascinating question regarding Rahab and Hebrews Chapter 11.

There's another intriguing fact from this story that demonstrates God's love for sinners. Since Rahab had become a believer, why then would God choose to record her name in the New Testament as "Rahab the prostitute" (Hebrews 11:31)? Why didn't He simply identify her as "Rahab the believer"? Was it not to demonstrate that He indeed is no respecter of persons and that all men and women everywhere can call on the name of the Lord and be saved (Romans 10:13)?[3]

Great question! Why is Rahab still labeled as a prostitute when she is in the Hall of Fame of Faith? I believe Getz brings out some great truths. Perhaps the label is still there to show that God's love abounds for whosoever will trust Him. Possibly Rahab is mentioned in Hebrews 11 to remind us of what God rescued her from. Our God can take a prostitute and turn that person into a permanent fixture in His Hall of Fame of Faith. God can take your faults and replace them with a growing faith in Him. He can turn your mistakes into His masterpieces. His grace makes way for His power to transform your life forever.

Questions:

1. In what ways is your faith growing stronger?
   How is this growth related to your focus on His grace?

2. Why do you think Rahab is still labeled as a prostitute in Hebrews 11?

3. How can you trust Him to take the world's label on you and replace it with His legacy for you?

Day Fifteen

Pictures of Grace

Grace in the Midst of Pain

In the midst of everything that unfolds in life, in the mystery of
His purpose, God sets His love and affection on unlikely people,
in unlikely contexts, doing routine things.
Alistair Begg[1]

The book of Ruth is a bright light in a dark world. It is no accident
that it appears where it does in Scripture.
Ruth follows Judges because this story so subtly yet so clearly
challenges the brooding stories that darken
and defile the pages preceding.
Michael Moore[2]

Text: Matthew 1:1, 5
¹ The book of the genealogy of Jesus Christ, the son of David,
the son of Abraham. . . . ⁵ and Salmon the father of Boaz by Rahab, and
Boaz the father of Obed by Ruth, and Obed the father of Jesse, . . .

Ruth 1:1-5
¹ In the days when the judges ruled there was a famine
in the land, and a man of Bethlehem in Judah went to sojourn
in the country of Moab, he and his wife and his two sons. ² The
name of the man was Elimelech and the name of his wife Naomi,
and the names of his two sons were Mahlon and Chilion. They
were Ephrathites from Bethlehem in Judah. They went into the
country of Moab and remained there. ³ But Elimelech, the husband
of Naomi, died, and she was left with her two sons. ⁴ These took

Moabite wives; the name of the one was Orpah and the name of the other Ruth. They lived there about ten years, ⁵ and both Mahlon and Chilion died, so that the woman was left without her two sons and her husband.

Thoughts:

The second half of Matthew 1:5 reveals another picture of grace. Her name is Ruth. Her entire grace story is depicted in an Old Testament book titled after her name. Many brilliant scholars have studied the book of Ruth. Take note of what a few of them had to say about this tiny book comprised of just eighty-five verses:

Alistair Begg shares this incredible insight into Ruth.

> So much is going on at this point in Israel's history, yet the focus of God is on a sad and lonely lady. This is the only book in the Bible entirely devoted to the domestic story of a woman. It shows the amazing compassion and empathy of God for the back streets and side alleys and the people who feel themselves to be last, lost, and left out. God says, 'The whole world is going on, but I am with you. I hem you in behind and before. I have set my hand upon you.' That is the kind of God we worship. [3]

Warren Wiersbe summarized the four chapters of Ruth as follows:

> He describes the first chapter of Ruth as the *weeping* chapter, the second as the *working* chapter, the third as the *waiting* chapter, and the fourth as the *wedding* chapter. Or, in other words, this is a story about the heart: first, about *broken* hearts; second,

about *comforted* hearts; third, about *assured* hearts; and fourth, about *joyful* hearts.[4]

Dr. Stephen Davey introduces his study of Ruth with these words:

> We will be introduced to a Gentile girl who is a descendant of Moab, condemned by God's law and even forbidden worship in God's temple: *"No Ammonite or Moabite shall enter the assembly of the LORD"* (Deuteronomy 23:3).
> Boaz will eventually redeem her (paralleling our own redemption), not because she met the requirements of the Law but because of his grace and love for her.
> The Law declared, "Keep out!" Grace exclaimed, "Welcome home!"[5]

While these eloquent words portray the beautiful story of redemption in Ruth, this story started with great loss and grief. "In the days when the judges ruled" reveals that the setting of the book of Ruth was in a dark time spiritually. Times were not just dark; they were desperate. A famine in Bethlehem drove Elimelech and his wife Naomi to a place called Moab. The name Bethlehem means "house of bread." Ironic that they had to leave the house of bread to find food! Such is the case many times in life. Hard times hit all people at some point in life. Well, for this couple searching for food, it is about to get a whole lot worse.

Elimelech dies and leaves Naomi as a widow with two sons. Both sons married Moabite women, because they were living in Moab. The two wives were named Orpah and Ruth. They stay in Moab for about ten years and then, both of the men die. So in Moab, Naomi has lost her husband and her two sons. All she has left are her daughters-in-law. Naomi's name in Hebrew means "pleasant" or "sweet." There is nothing pleasant about her life at this point. She is going through the intense grief of losing three family members extremely close to her while she is living in a foreign land.

What do you do when you feel like you have lost everything? Where do you turn when your life hits rock bottom? We need the God of grace, not only because we are sinners, but because we live in a world full of pain and grief. Great grief can bring both remarkable pain and a renewed perspective. Iain Campbell's commentary on Ruth gives a unique view of this topic:

> Until Jesus Christ fills the void in the heart of man, there will always be sorrow and heartache, there will always be meaningless and futility, and men will always wake up and say, 'What is it all for?' The world will continue to deceive and delude, to promise and to renege on its promises. Without a relationship with Jesus Christ, men will chase their dreams and pursue their plans down every road and every avenue of human experience, and they will always return saying, 'I did not find it there. I went down this road looking for peace and meaning and satisfaction, looking for purpose, and at the end of it there was brokenness—there were broken plans and broken dreams.'[6]

Sometimes we discover that Jesus is all we need when He is all we have. Jesus is not only our Savior; He is also our resurrection and life. He not only takes dead things and brings them back to life again; He is also the giver of our next breath and grants our next heartbeat. Will you trust Him daily and find the grace you need for dealing with all that this life entails?

Questions:

1. In what specific ways can you learn to trust God with the uncertainties and details of life?

2. How do you deal with grief as you trust God for His grace?

3. In this lesson you read the following in a quote by Dr. Stephen Davey: "The Law declared, 'Keep out!' Grace exclaimed, 'Welcome home!'" What is your opinion of this quote?

Day Sixteen

Pictures of Grace

In Pursuit of Grace

Here are three widows with three different ways of
handling the pain of life that they just couldn't avoid.
Orpah departs—her shallow faith based on circumstances.
Naomi returns—her weak faith biased by circumstances.
And Ruth arrives—her new faith seeing beyond circumstances.
Heading for a strange new land,
Ruth has a tight grip on her true and living God.
Dr. Stephen Davey[1]

Text: Ruth 1:6-22

[6] Then she arose with her daughters-in-law to return from
the country of Moab, for she had heard in the fields of Moab
that the Lord had visited his people and given them food. [7] So
she set out from the place where she was with her two daughters-in-law, and they went on the way to return to the land
of Judah. [8] But Naomi said to her two daughters-in-law, "Go,
return each of you to her mother's house. May the Lord deal
kindly with you, as you have dealt with the dead and with
me. [9] The Lord grant that you may find rest, each of you in the
house of her husband!" Then she kissed them, and they lifted
up their voices and wept. [10] And they said to her, "No, we will
return with you to your people."

[11] But Naomi said, "Turn back, my daughters; why will
you go with me? Have I yet sons in my womb that they may
become your husbands? [12] Turn back, my daughters; go your
way, for I am too old to have a husband. If I should say I have

58

hope, even if I should have a husband this night and should bear sons, ¹³ would you therefore wait till they were grown? Would you therefore refrain from marrying? No, my daughters, for it is exceedingly bitter to me for your sake that the hand of the Lord has gone out against me." ¹⁴ Then they lifted up their voices and wept again. And Orpah kissed her mother-in-law, but Ruth clung to her.

¹⁵ And she said, "See, your sister-in-law has gone back to her people and to her gods; return after your sister-in-law." ¹⁶ But Ruth said, "Do not urge me to leave you or to return from following you. For where you go I will go, and where you lodge I will lodge. Your people shall be my people, and your God my God.¹⁷ Where you die I will die, and there will I be buried. May the Lord do so to me and more also if anything but death parts me from you." ¹⁸ And when Naomi saw that she was determined to go with her, she said no more.

¹⁹ So the two of them went on until they came to Bethlehem. And when they came to Bethlehem, the whole town was stirred because of them. And the women said, "Is this Naomi?" ²⁰ She said to them, "Do not call me Naomi; call me Mara, for the Almighty has dealt very bitterly with me.

²¹ I went away full, and the Lord has brought me back empty. Why call me Naomi, when the Lord has testified against me and the Almighty has brought calamity upon me?"

²² So Naomi returned, and Ruth the Moabite her daughter-in-law with her, who returned from the country of Moab. And they came to Bethlehem at the beginning of barley harvest.

Thoughts:

Naomi has lost her husband and two sons in Moab. It is hard to stay in a place that you equate with pain. Naomi tells Orpah and Ruth goodbye and intends to go back to Bethlehem alone. She heard that the physical famine is over in Bethlehem, and she wants to leave Moab and go back home. God's Word says that "Orpah kissed her mother-in-law." Orpah said goodbye. But verse 14 states that "Ruth clung to her." Ruth decided to stay with Naomi.

Alistair Begg expresses the emotions that must have been going through Ruth's mind as she made that life-changing decision.

> It is fascinating that the same fact that caused Orpah to return caused Ruth to stay. Orpah processed Naomi's childlessness and decided that she would leave, desiring to become a wife. Ruth processed the information and decided that she would stay, committed to being a daughter. The same circumstances, the same information, a momentous decision: 'Wherever you go, I'm there.'
>
> Ruth wasn't just agreeing to go on a short-term mission project. Her statement means goodbye to Orpah, goodbye to familiarity, goodbye to everything that has meant security to her, and hello to the great unknown. She was choosing an uncertain future as a widow in a land where she knew no-one. She was agreeing to stay with Naomi, 'till death do us part'. Even in death she promises to be buried with Naomi's people; that's a huge commitment. And her deep conviction came not only because of Naomi herself, but also on account of Naomi's God.
>
> God is still looking for people of deep conviction, those who will nurture a 'till death do us part' kind of commitment.[2]

Ruth's commitment is inspiring. Her words in verse 16 have encouraged people for over 2,000 years. Ruth told Naomi, "Do not urge me to leave you or to return from following you. For where you go I will go, and where you lodge I will lodge. Your people shall be my people, and your God my God." Countless multitudes of people have used Ruth's statement for years at weddings.

But Dr. Stephen Davey said, "She has absolutely nothing to gain by going with Naomi ... and she has everything to lose. The most remote thing in her future is the sound of wedding bells." Davey goes on to add the following:

> Ruth tells Naomi that no matter what the future holds and no matter where their future takes them, she will stay by her side. This is no snap decision—no whim or sudden impulse. Ruth knows that Naomi has nothing to offer her except poverty and hardship.
>
> ... We've read this story so often that we've forgotten what Ruth is giving up. She's already lost her husband. Now she's turning her back on her citizenship, her country, her family, her religion, and her security.
>
> She is literally giving away her future.[3]

Another author put it this way:

> Ruth possesses nothing. No deity has promised her blessing; no human being has come to her aid. She lives and chooses without a support system, and she knows that the fruit of her decision may well be the emptiness of rejection and, perhaps, even death. She has committed herself to an older widow rather than search for a new husband. There is no more radical decision in all the memories of Israel.[4]

Questions:

1. Re-read Dr. Stephen Davey's quote at the beginning of this lesson. Of the descriptions provided in Davey's quote, which widow resembles your normal response to pain? Why?

2. What can you learn from Ruth's response?

3. List some specific ways you can pursue grace in your walk with Jesus.

Day Seventeen

Pictures of Grace

Under the Wings of His Grace

How precious is Your steadfast love, O God!
The children of mankind take refuge
in the shadow of Your wings.
Psalm 36:7

. . . for in You my soul takes refuge;
in the shadow of Your wings I will take refuge,
till the storms of destruction pass by.
Psalm 57:1

Text: Ruth 2:1-23

[1] Now Naomi had a relative of her husband's, a worthy man of the clan of Elimelech, whose name was Boaz. [2] And Ruth the Moabite said to Naomi, "Let me go to the field and glean among the ears of grain after him in whose sight I shall find favor." And she said to her, "Go, my daughter." [3] So she set out and went and gleaned in the field after the reapers, and she happened to come to the part of the field belonging to Boaz, who was of the clan of Elimelech. [4] And behold, Boaz came from Bethlehem. And he said to the reapers, "The Lord be with you!" And they answered, "The Lord bless you." [5] Then Boaz said to his young man who was in charge of the reapers, "Whose young woman is this?" [6] And the servant who was in charge of the reapers answered, "She is the young Moabite woman, who came back with Naomi from the country of Moab. [7] She said, 'Please let me glean and gather among the sheaves after the reapers.'

So she came, and she has continued from early morning until now, except for a short rest."

⁸ Then Boaz said to Ruth, "Now, listen, my daughter, do not go to glean in another field or leave this one, but keep close to my young women. ⁹ Let your eyes be on the field that they are reaping, and go after them. Have I not charged the young men not to touch you? And when you are thirsty, go to the vessels and drink what the young men have drawn." ¹⁰ Then she fell on her face, bowing to the ground, and said to him, "Why have I found favor in your eyes, that you should take notice of me, since I am a foreigner?" ¹¹ But Boaz answered her, "All that you have done for your mother-in-law since the death of your husband has been fully told to me, and how you left your father and mother and your native land and came to a people that you did not know before. ¹² The Lord repay you for what you have done, and a full reward be given you by the Lord, the God of Israel, under whose wings you have come to take refuge!" ¹³ Then she said, "I have found favor in your eyes, my lord, for you have comforted me and spoken kindly to your servant, though I am not one of your servants."

¹⁴ And at mealtime Boaz said to her, "Come here and eat some bread and dip your morsel in the wine." So she sat beside the reapers, and he passed to her roasted grain. And she ate until she was satisfied, and she had some left over. ¹⁵ When she rose to glean, Boaz instructed his young men, saying, "Let her glean even among the sheaves, and do not reproach her. ¹⁶ And also pull out some from the bundles for her and leave it for her to glean, and do not rebuke her."

¹⁷ So she gleaned in the field until evening. Then she beat out what she had gleaned, and it was about an ephah of barley. ¹⁸ And she took it up and went into the city. Her mother-in-law saw what she had gleaned. She also brought out and gave her what food she had left over after being satisfied. ¹⁹ And

her mother-in-law said to her, "Where did you glean today? And where have you worked? Blessed be the man who took notice of you." So she told her mother-in-law with whom she had worked and said, "The man's name with whom I worked today is Boaz." [20] And Naomi said to her daughter-in-law, "May he be blessed by the Lord, whose kindness has not forsaken the living or the dead!" Naomi also said to her, "The man is a close relative of ours, one of our redeemers." [21] And Ruth the Moabite said, "Besides, he said to me, 'You shall keep close by my young men until they have finished all my harvest.'" [22] And Naomi said to Ruth, her daughter-in-law, "It is good, my daughter, that you go out with his young women, lest in another field you be assaulted." [23] So she kept close to the young women of Boaz, gleaning until the end of the barley and wheat harvests. And she lived with her mother-in-law.

Thoughts:

In the second chapter of Ruth, we are introduced to Boaz. His name comes from a Hebrew root word that means, "to be strong." He will be the redeemer in Ruth's life because God, the Redeemer, is leading them both by His grace.

God is leading them to each other at the precise time orchestrated by His divine plan. It is harvest time!

We come now to another interesting and significant detail in the story. The return of Naomi and Ruth was in the beginning of the *harvest*. It was the time of reaping toward the end of the season. The sowing time was past, and the time for the final reaping had come. Soon the time for threshing would be here and the rejoicing of the harvest festival. The time of Naomi's return is significant, as well as the gleaning of Ruth till the end of the harvest.[1]

God's hand of grace is all over this encounter.

Iain Campbell's commentary adds some very important details.

> This chapter tells us a very interesting thing about Ruth: she occupies a two-fold position at this point. We are told in verse twelve of this chapter that she has a place *under the wings of God*. (2:12). We know from Chapter One and the events that unfolded in Moab and on the road to Bethlehem that Ruth had indeed turned her back on Moab with all its gods and idols, to put her trust in the one living and true God. She had come to trust under the wings of the Lord God of Israel, and because she was under the wings of Jehovah, she was also *gleaning in the fields of Boaz*. (2:17).
>
> It is important that we see the link between these two things. There is an intimate connection between them. Under the wings of Jehovah, she is enjoying a provision that is given to her in the fields of Boaz. God has brought her to put her trust personally in himself, in Jehovah, the Lord God of the covenant. God shows that his blessing is upon Ruth by making this rich provision to her when she comes into these particular fields to glean and to gather corn. Under the wings of God and in the fields of Boaz is where Ruth's provision is found.[2]

Ruth doesn't know it at the time, but God is working His will for her good all because of His grace!

There are hints of Boaz' commitment to Ruth in his comments to her. The verb translated "come here" or "stay" is the same verb translated "clung" in 1:14. Boaz wants Ruth to cling to him as tightly as she now clings to Naomi.[3] Boaz makes it clear throughout this chapter that he is extremely interested in Ruth. God's favor and blessing is all over Ruth and Naomi's situation. They are both finding refuge under His wings!

Questions:

1. If you were completely honest with yourself, what have you clung to the most in your life?

2. Does your answer above give you true confidence or false security? Why or why not?

3. Meditate and envision yourself under the shadow of His wings. As you imagine being under the wings of His grace, what emotions stir in your soul?

Day Eighteen

Pictures of Grace

Grace through Faith

Faith is to believe what you do not see;
the reward of this faith is to see what you believe.
St. Augustine[1]

Faith and obedience are bound up in the same bundle;
he that obeys God trusts God; and he that trusts God obeys God.
He that is without faith is without works,
and he that is without works is without faith.
Charles Haddon Spurgeon[2]

Text: Ruth 3:1-18

[1] Then Naomi, her mother-in-law, said to her, "My daughter, should I not seek rest for you, that it may be well with you? [2] Is not Boaz our relative, with whose young women you were? See, he is winnowing barley tonight at the threshing floor. [3] Wash therefore and anoint yourself, and put on your cloak and go down to the threshing floor, but do not make yourself known to the man until he has finished eating and drinking. [4] But when he lies down, observe the place where he lies. Then go and uncover his feet and lie down, and he will tell you what to do." [5] And she replied, "All that you say I will do."

[6] So she went down to the threshing floor and did just as her mother-in-law had commanded her. [7] And when Boaz had eaten and drunk, and his heart was merry, he went to lie down at the end of the heap of grain. Then she came softly and uncovered his feet and lay down. [8] At midnight the man was startled and

turned over, and behold, a woman lay at his feet! [9] He said, "Who are you?" And she answered, "I am Ruth, your servant. Spread your wings over your servant, for you are a redeemer." [10] And he said, "May you be blessed by the Lord, my daughter. You have made this last kindness greater than the first in that you have not gone after young men, whether poor or rich. [11] And now, my daughter, do not fear. I will do for you all that you ask, for all my fellow townsmen know that you are a worthy woman. [12] And now it is true that I am a redeemer. Yet there is a redeemer nearer than I. [13] Remain tonight, and in the morning, if he will redeem you, good; let him do it. But if he is not willing to redeem you, then, as the Lord lives, I will redeem you. Lie down until the morning."

[14] So she lay at his feet until the morning, but arose before one could recognize another. And he said, "Let it not be known that the woman came to the threshing floor." [15] And he said, "Bring the garment you are wearing and hold it out." So she held it, and he measured out six measures of barley and put it on her. Then she went into the city. [16] And when she came to her mother-in-law, she said, "How did you fare, my daughter?" Then she told her all that the man had done for her, [17] saying, "These six measures of barley he gave to me, for he said to me, 'You must not go back empty-handed to your mother-in-law.'" [18] She replied, "Wait, my daughter, until you learn how the matter turns out, for the man will not rest but will settle the matter today."

Thoughts:

Have you ever looked back over your life thoughtfully and admired the hand of God at work? There are reflective seasons of my life where I am fully aware that all I have in this life is because God brought me grace. I had a desire to serve Him and speak into the lives of others, and now I have been in the ministry for four decades. God placed that desire in my heart and led me to the events that placed me in His perfect will. Then I felt called to move to another town and serve Him. So, I accepted that call and followed Him. God knew that I would meet my future spouse there. Following His will in one decision allowed me to be where I needed to be so that I could follow Him in another one.

I don't believe in coincidences. I call them instead, "God-instances." There are instances in all our lives that God in His sovereignty places there. God works in the details in the lives of His children. Yet, He loves His children unconditionally and gives them free will to choose to follow Him.

I am fully mindful that my decisions in life have consequences, both good and bad. I have always said, "Your life is the sum total of the choices you make." If you make good choices, you will have good consequences. And vice versa. If you are reaping a good harvest currently, it is because you planted good seed at some point in the past and God blessed it. If you are experiencing a bad harvest, it could be the fruit of bad decisions. But make no mistake, our decisions matter. For example, you decide to move to a certain city. Not only will it affect you, but also your children and their future decisions.

Naomi and Ruth find themselves in the balance between God's purpose and plan for their lives and their decision to follow Him. God brought the famine to an end in Bethlehem, so Naomi went back to her hometown. Ruth had the choice to stay where she was in Moab, or commit to stay by the side of her mother-in-law. She chose to stay with Naomi. That choice put her at the threshing floor of Boaz' field, where he met her. Now Boaz has blessed her with food and showed his personal interest. Ruth is under the shadow of God's wings and in the view of Boaz' attention.

Grace and works do go hand in hand. God gives the grace, but we have to choose to follow Him. So Naomi comes up with a plan. In Ruth 3:1, Naomi basically says, "Ruth, we need to get you a husband."

M.R. De Haan explains what happens next:

> To the unspiritual mind this suggestion of Naomi was entirely out of place, but when we understand the motive and the faith of Naomi, it becomes the story of a faith that would not be denied. After the harvest was ended, the sheaves were brought to the threshing floor to be winnowed. This was done at night to get the advantage of the night breezes which sprang up after dark in that country and which were needed to successfully fan the grain, to separate it from the chaff. The grain would first be beaten out of its husk and separated from the straw. Then the grain was picked up and cast up into the wind. The heavier grain would fall onto the threshing floor, while the lighter chaff would be blown away. After the grain had been thus winnowed and the winds subsided about midnight, a sumptuous meal was served and then all retired.
>
> The owner of the grain would then remain on the scene and lie down at the side of the heap of winnowed grain to guard it against thieves who would otherwise steal it. And so, Boaz after the meal lay down at the pile of grain. Naomi was fully familiar with this harvest and threshing routine, and so she instructed Ruth to wait until the lights were all out, and the floor was quiet, and then to steal softly to the place where Boaz was sleeping, uncover his feet and lie down.[3]

And, like they say, "the rest is history." Well, it is His story at work in the lives of two women who acted in faith.

Questions:

1. How is your faith in God expressed in your works for God?

2. George Mueller once said, "The beginning of anxiety is the end of faith, and the beginning of true faith is the end of anxiety."[4] How does this quote relate to today's Scripture? How can you apply the truth of this statement in your life by faith?

Day Nineteen

Pictures of Grace

Redeeming Grace

The Book of Ruth provides the only detailed example in the
Bible of the Hebrew *goel*—kinsman redeemer.
Stephen Davey[1]

The Book of Ruth declares that redemption is
not a business transaction. . . it is a love story.
J. Vernon McGee[2]

Text: Ruth 4:1-12

[1] Now Boaz had gone up to the gate and sat down there.
And behold, the redeemer, of whom Boaz had spoken, came
by. So Boaz said, "Turn aside, friend; sit down here." And
he turned aside and sat down. [2] And he took ten men of
the elders of the city and said, "Sit down here." So they sat
down. [3] Then he said to the redeemer, "Naomi, who has come
back from the country of Moab, is selling the parcel of land
that belonged to our relative Elimelech. [4] So I thought I would
tell you of it and say, 'Buy it in the presence of those sitting
here and in the presence of the elders of my people.' If you
will redeem it, redeem it. But if you will not, tell me, that I
may know, for there is no one besides you to redeem it, and
I come after you." And he said, "I will redeem it." [5] Then Boaz
said, "The day you buy the field from the hand of Naomi,
you also acquire Ruth the Moabite, the widow of the dead, in
order to perpetuate the name of the dead in his inheritance."
[6] Then the redeemer said, "I cannot redeem it for myself, lest

73

I impair my own inheritance. Take my right of redemption yourself, for I cannot redeem it."

⁷ Now this was the custom in former times in Israel concerning redeeming and exchanging: to confirm a transaction, the one drew off his sandal and gave it to the other, and this was the manner of attesting in Israel. ⁸ So when the redeemer said to Boaz, "Buy it for yourself," he drew off his sandal. ⁹ Then Boaz said to the elders and all the people, "You are witnesses this day that I have bought from the hand of Naomi all that belonged to Elimelech and all that belonged to Chilion and to Mahlon. ¹⁰ Also Ruth the Moabite, the widow of Mahlon, I have bought to be my wife, to perpetuate the name of the dead in his inheritance, that the name of the dead may not be cut off from among his brothers and from the gate of his native place. You are witnesses this day." ¹¹ Then all the people who were at the gate and the elders said, "We are witnesses. May the Lord make the woman, who is coming into your house, like Rachel and Leah, who together built up the house of Israel. May you act worthily in Ephrathah and be renowned in Bethlehem, ¹² and may your house be like the house of Perez, whom Tamar bore to Judah, because of the offspring that the Lord will give you by this young woman."

Thoughts:

Today, we come to the greatest example of a redeemer in the Old Testament. M. R. De Haan reinforces this by stating,

> Here we see Boaz, the Bethlehemite, calling an assembly of the elders of the city to present himself in the role of a Redeemer. It is the clearest type of the Lord Jesus Christ as the Redeemer of His people to be found anywhere in the Scripture.³

It would be an understatement to say that this section of Scripture is extremely important in our spiritual understanding of grace. De Haan's commentary gives a clear summary.

> To truly appreciate the story of Ruth's redemption by Boaz we must understand the Scriptural meaning of the words, "redeem, redeemer and redemption." The word translated "redeem" in the Old Testament is "gaal" and means to "buy back," or to set free. It is the act whereby when, after a person's property or his liberty had been forfeited to another, it could be bought back again upon the payment of the legal price set by the law. Thus, if one had lost title to a home or piece of land, the law made provision whereby at any time it could be bought back again. Today it may be compared to "pawning" one's property with the privilege of redeeming it later. This law also applied to a slave who had sold himself for debts or other obligations, but could be redeemed and set free. A third application of the law of redemption was for childless widows. If a husband died without leaving a child, then the husband's brother was to take his deceased brother's wife and raise up his name in Israel. This was the law of redemption of property, people, and widows.
>
> All these three aspects of redemption are found in the Book of Ruth. Naomi and Ruth had lost claim to the estate of Elimelech, through Naomi's absence and default. She had forfeited her claim to the family estate. This was subject to redemption. Ruth also had lost her liberty, for she was a Gentile outcast and outside the covenant blessing of Israel. This could only be redeemed, as she was accepted in the family of God's people by her marriage to Boaz. But she was also a widow and needed a kinsman-redeemer.[4]

The application of this Scripture is reinforced by Iain Campbell's commentary.

> All Ruth's interests focus now on one single individual. There are many men in Bethlehem-Judah, many field owners and others coming and going at the time of harvest, but there is only one man who can provide the hope and the security that Ruth needs. All that will be done by way of redemption focuses exclusively on that one person. This is a point that has been emphasized time and again in the course of this great Old Testament book.
> It is also a point that is echoed in the Gospel. Jesus Christ will not share His position as Redeemer with any other. Every sinner who ever came into his Kingdom and who ever found salvation and liberty through the Gospel of the Lord Jesus Christ found it because He became their everything and their all.[5]

The Book of Ruth is significant to our understanding of grace. Because of its importance, it became an essential section of Scripture in the life of God's people.

> In the Hebrew culture, Ruth was one of five scrolls that would be read annually at a Jewish festival. Other scrolls read were Esther at the Feast of Purim, Ecclesiastes at the Feast of Tabernacles, and Ruth at the Feast of Weeks, also known as Pentecost.
> It isn't a coincidence that the love story of a kinsman redeemer winning his bride would be read at the Feast of Pentecost where, centuries later, *the* Kinsman Redeemer initiated the redeeming of His Bride as the Church was created.[6]

Questions:

1. How is God's timing in this story a display of both His perfect sovereignty and His matchless grace?

2. How is Boaz a great picture of Jesus as our personal redeemer?

3. What is significant about the book of Ruth being read at the Feast of Pentecost?

Pictures of Grace

Restoring Grace

The LORD has not promised us a world without hardship, but that, in the midst of hardship, He will be revealed through us.
Francis Frangipane[1]

Moab signifies death, emptiness and no sons.
Bethlehem signifies life, fullness and sons.
Daniel Hawk[2]

Text: Ruth 4:13-17

[13] So Boaz took Ruth, and she became his wife. And he went in to her, and the Lord gave her conception, and she bore a son. [14] Then the women said to Naomi, "Blessed be the Lord, who has not left you this day without a redeemer, and may his name be renowned in Israel! [15] He shall be to you a restorer of life and a nourisher of your old age, for your daughter-in-law who loves you, who is more to you than seven sons, has given birth to him." [16] Then Naomi took the child and laid him on her lap and became his nurse. [17] And the women of the neighborhood gave him a name, saying, "A son has been born to Naomi." They named him Obed. He was the father of Jesse, the father of David.

Thoughts:

Our God is a God of restoration. A worldly definition of restoration is "the act of returning something to its previous state." It could be defined as "making something new again." Yet a biblical definition of restoration is "transforming something into a better condition than it existed in its previous state." The New Testament word for restoration can even mean a rebirth.

Let's look at just a few examples of biblical restoration. Jeremiah 30:17 speaks of physical restoration. "For I will restore health to you, and your wounds I will heal, declares the Lord." David cries out for spiritual restoration in Psalm 51:12. "Restore to me the joy of Your salvation, and uphold me with a willing spirit." Restoration can occur in our situations and circumstances. Job 42:10 states, "And the Lord restored the fortunes of Job, when he prayed for his friends. And the Lord gave Job twice as much as he had before." The New Living Version of Romans 5:10 reveals the restoration provided by Jesus our Redeemer. "For since our friendship with God was restored by the death of His Son while we were still His enemies, we will certainly be saved through the life of His Son." Restoration is the overarching theme of Scripture, and it is the frame around the picture of grace in the story of Ruth.

Daniel Hawk discusses this restoration for Ruth by giving the following contrast.

> Naomi travels with her family to Moab, and all her men die there. In her own words she was 'full' when she left Bethlehem but comes back 'empty' from Moab (1:21a). She loses her sons in Moab (1:5) but gains a son in Bethlehem (Obed, 4:17), not to mention a daughter-in-law worth more than seven sons (4:15). Departing from Bethlehem brings woe and separation. Returning to Bethlehem brings fulfilment and restoration.[3]

Dr. Stephen Davey gives his description of restoration in Ruth with these words.

The Book of Ruth opens with three funerals but closes with a wedding… and a baby boy. There is a good deal of weeping recorded in the first chapter, but the last is filled with overflowing joy. Now, not all of life's events have a happy ending, but this little book reminds the Christian, especially, that it is God who writes the last chapter.[4]

It is extremely encouraging to know that our God of restoration has the final word.

Ruth 4:14-15 records what turns out to be a divine blessing. A group of women said these prophetic words to Naomi, "Blessed be the Lord, who has not left you this day without a redeemer, and may his name be renowned in Israel! He shall be to you a restorer of life and a nourisher of your old age, for your daughter-in-law who loves you, who is more to you than seven sons, has given birth to him." Did you catch that phrase, "restorer of life"? Our God restores and blesses for the glory and honor of His name.

Iain Campbell's commentary gives abundant insight on these verses of Scripture.

So the blessing of God's love, of God's purpose was clear in the family of Boaz. There was also going to be the blessing of worth and fame: 'May you prosper in Ephrathah and be famous in Bethlehem' (4:11; NLT). Maybe there were some that didn't know of Boaz and Ruth. But Ruth's name was going to become famous. In the experience of the people of God at the time, she was going to be famous in Bethlehem because she belonged to the household of Boaz. Long after she is gone, and her dust mingles with the dust of the earth, her fame continues because her story is written with the finger of God.

The world is full of men and women who are desperately searching for something by which to be remembered. Their one great aim is to be on everybody's lips, their consuming passion is that men will remember them long after they are gone, that men will remember what they did, and what they said, and the contribution they made in their own field. But everything about us here will pass away, except what God has done and been for us in Christ. Every name that has ever been written in the books of men will vanish, but those that have been written in the Lamb's book of life, written with the finger of God, in his inerrant record of the ages, their name, bound up with the name of their kinsman-redeemer, will live on beyond death in immortal annals. What matters ultimately is not whether men will remember us when we're gone. What matters is whether our name is written in the Lamb's book of life.[5]

Our God restores and blesses. He redeems and heals. God does what He does because He is who He is. His merciful actions stem from His matchless nature. May our lives be a testimony of His restoring power and infinite mercy. Even if He chooses to bless us, it will be for His glory for He alone is the Famous One.

Questions:

1. In what specific way is God restoring you?

2. How do you see His hand of mercy and grace on your life today?

3. How is your life inspired by knowing God has the final word?

4. How do David's words in Psalm 30:5 apply to the story of Ruth and to your life personally? *"Weeping may tarry for the night, but joy comes with the morning."*

Day Twenty-One

Pictures of Grace

God of Judgment and Grace

Redemption is the "payment of a debt or obligation."
There were notes, warrants held against us. We are all debtors
to God, but by His death on the cross Jesus satisfied the
warrants held against us. The moment you accepted Jesus
into your heart, all the things you ever did wrong—every
evil thought, every angry word, and every wicked deed,
each of which deserved its own punishment—were stamped
REDEEMED: PAID IN FULL by our Father in Heaven.
Jesus paid for them all with His blood. He is our Redeemer.
Francis Frangipane[1]

Text: Ruth 4:18-22
[18] Now these are the generations of Perez: Perez fathered
Hezron, [19] Hezron fathered Ram, Ram fathered Amminadab,
[20] Amminadab fathered Nahshon, Nahshon fathered Salmon, [21] Salmon fathered Boaz, Boaz fathered Obed,[22] Obed
fathered Jesse, and Jesse fathered David.

Thoughts:
These last few verses in Ruth seem to be a simple
genealogy. But God's Word is always more than just mere
words on a page. Every word is valuable because all Scripture
is inspired by God to bring wisdom into our lives. I will leave
the depth of this discussion to one much wiser than myself -
M. R. De Hann:

Here the story should have ended, but instead there is added a genealogy... the Holy Spirit added the closing five verses for a very definite purpose.

Strange ending indeed for a love story! Just a fragmentary genealogy, a single branch from a family tree! There are just ten names in this list, beginning with Perez, son of Judah, and ending with David, king of Israel. It begins with an [illegitimate child] and ends with a great king. It is the story of Grace, Grace, Grace, - the story of a poor, unworthy Gentile widow becoming the happy bride of the wealthy Boaz. But the brief genealogy is for an additional reason, to show the righteousness and justice of God.

To illustrate the justice of God, David was the first man in Israel who had a right to Israel's throne. He was a descendant of Perez, the illegitimate son of Judah. We have the sordid record in Genesis 38.[2]

Remember Tamar from our first picture of grace in the genealogy of Jesus. Tamar had twins through a deceitful strategy to trick her father-in-law into sleeping with her. One of those twins was named Perez, who is mentioned here in Ruth. (I love how God ties the pictures of His grace into an art gallery of His goodness!)

The significance of all this will become evident as we see God's provision. The genealogy begins, therefore, with Perez, and then there follow nine names, making a total of ten—just ten. No more. No less. Just ten: Perez, Hezron, Ram, Amminadab, Nahshon, Salmon, Boaz, Obed, Jesse, and David. Exactly ten in number! Jesse, the father of David, the king, was the ninth, and David himself was the tenth.

Believing as we do in the infallible inspiration of the Scriptures, we immediately look for a reason for this strange ending in the Book of Ruth. We have the answer given, however, when we turn to Deuteronomy 23, verse 2. Here is God's own commandment regarding the situation of an illegitimate child:

"No one born of a forbidden union may enter the assembly of the Lord. Even to the tenth generation, none of his descendants may enter the assembly of the Lord."

Here is the definite command of the Lord that no child born out of wedlock should ever be admitted into Israel until the tenth generation. Nine is thought to be the number of judgment, and the judgment of sin must first be fulfilled. Only after nine generations may a person, therefore, who is a descendant born of this unholy practice, take his place in testimony, for ten is the number of testimony.

The expression, "no one born of forbidden union may enter the assembly of the Lord," had reference to a place in the royal line of Israel. It did not imply being a social outcast. Ancient rabbis interpreted it to mean that no descendant of an illegitimate child could sit upon the throne of Israel until the tenth generation. This seems to be the correct meaning as recorded in the actual history of Israel.

God never departs from His Word, and generations afterward He keeps His command. It was, therefore, impossible for any of the descendants of Perez to sit on Israel's throne for ten generations, and when Israel under Samuel demanded a king, God could not give them a legitimate king from the royal tribe of Judah, because the curse of Deuteronomy 23:2 still rested upon them. When Israel demanded a king, it was only the ninth generation since Perez, the son of sin, the son of Judah. Jesse, who was then in the line, was only the ninth. David was the tenth, but was not yet ready, probably not yet born. Since the curse of ten generations was upon the line of Judah, the kingly line, until David should be ready for the work of the Lord, God could not honor the request of Israel for a king and so He steps outside the tribe of Judah into the tribe of Benjamin, and gives them Saul, the son of Kish, instead.

Considering all of this, can you deny or doubt the supernatural, infallible inspiration of the Scriptures? If I personally had no other evidence of the supernatural authorship of this wonderful Book than this closing genealogy in Ruth, it would be entirely enough for me.[3]

Wow, what insight from De Haan. And I love that last quote. Just this one instance in Scripture is enough for us to understand that God's Word is infallible, and that God obeys His own Word. God always keeps His Word (Scripture), while at the same time, He restores and redeems His children through His grace.

This balance of judgment and grace is why God sent His Son Jesus. Only in Jesus Christ, our spotless Passover Lamb, could God righteously pay the penalty for our sin and save those who would put their trust in Him. That's why we call it "Saving Grace."

Questions:

1. God is both a God of His Word and God of grace. How does His balance of both create in you more of an admiration for who He is?

2. How does Jesus coming to fulfill the law become the greatest picture of grace?

3. What are your thoughts on the following statement from today's devotion? "God never departs from His Word, and generations afterward He keeps His command."

Day Twenty-Two

Pictures of Grace

Sin's Entrapment

The place of our location has much to do
with the purity of our life.
John G. Butler[1]

The power that brought David down was not an external enemy.
King David was not safe from himself. The walls of Jerusalem
were no protection against his own deep flaws.
John Woodhouse[2]

Text: Matthew 1:1, 6
[1] The book of the genealogy of Jesus Christ, the son of
David, the son of Abraham. . . [6] and Jesse the father of David the
king. And David was the father of Solomon by the wife of Uriah, . . .

2 Samuel 11:1-5
[1] In the spring of the year, the time when kings go out to battle,
David sent Joab, and his servants with him, and all Israel. And
they ravaged the Ammonites and besieged Rabbah. But David
remained at Jerusalem. [2] It happened, late one afternoon, when
David arose from his couch and was walking on the roof of the
king's house, that he saw from the roof a woman bathing; and
the woman was very beautiful. [3] And David sent and inquired
about the woman. And one said, "Is not this Bathsheba, the
daughter of Eliam, the wife of Uriah the Hittite?" [4] So David sent
messengers and took her, and she came to him, and he lay with
her. (Now she had been purifying herself from her uncleanness).

Then she returned to her house. ⁵ And the woman conceived, and she sent and told David, "I am pregnant."

Thoughts:

You can't reflect on the life of David in Scripture, and not be automatically reminded of two names: Goliath and Bathsheba. When you think about David's life, your mind instinctively goes back to his greatest victory and his worst sins. In fact, Pastor James Merritt said the following about David's sin with Bathsheba, "No single sin outside the sin that Adam and Eve committed in the Garden of Eden, has received more press coverage than David with Bathsheba." I agree.

Yet, while this Scripture has had much attention, it still has a lot of spiritual lessons that most don't discuss. While many people focus on David, what happens with Bathsheba doesn't get much consideration. Even in Matthew's account of the genealogy of Jesus, her name is not mentioned: ". . . by the wife of Uriah." Therefore, in these next several days, we will look at life lessons from both David and Bathsheba, as we continue looking at God's pictures of grace.

We notice from the beginning of 2 Samuel 11, that David sent his men to war, yet he stayed in Jerusalem. Many scholars have pointed out that David wasn't where he was supposed to be when his downfall began. Warren Wiersbe noted:

"Satan finds some mischief for idle hands to do." Idleness isn't just the absence of activity, for all of us need regular rest; idleness is also activity to no purpose. When David was finished with his afternoon nap, he should have immediately moved into some kingdom duty that would have occupied his mind and body, or, if he wanted to take a walk, he should have invited someone to walk with him. "If you are idle, be not solitary," wrote Samuel

Johnson; "if you are solitary, be not idle." Had David followed that counsel, he would have saved himself and his family a great deal of heartache.

When David laid aside his armor, he took the first step toward moral defeat, and the same principle applies to believers today (Eph. 6:10—18). Without the helmet of salvation, we don't think like saved people; and without the breastplate of righteousness, we have nothing to protect the heart. Lacking the belt of truth, we easily believe lies ("We can get away with this!"), and without the sword of the Word and the shield of faith, we are helpless before the Enemy. Without prayer we have no power. As for the shoes of peace, David walked in the midst of battles for the rest of his life. He was safer on the battlefield than in his own house![3]

Therefore, David is not where he should have been when temptation entered his mind.

Now, let's look at Bathsheba. I have always thought that Bathsheba tempted David and that she was partly to blame. But as I have studied and researched others, I believe that I have been completely wrong. David can't blame his sin on Bathsheba just because she was taking a bath. Here is what I learned.

The narrator in 2 Samuel 11 places the blame squarely on David, showing Bathsheba as a victim, not the aggressor. In the biblical story, David is the one making decision after decision to drive himself and his kingdom toward destruction. By paying careful attention to the story in 2 Samuel 11 and the other passages where she appears in Scripture, we see a different characterization of Bathsheba. We can come to understand something about what Matthew meant in including her in Jesus' genealogy.[4]

It was not unusual for Bathsheba to bathe outside, since there was no indoor plumbing. David, who likely owned the tallest of all the surrounding buildings, goes atop his roof to enjoy the natural air conditioning and, while there, he sees a woman below bathing. Despite the commentary of preachers through the centuries, nothing in the passage indicates the woman's reason for choosing that spot to bathe. In fact, we have nothing to suggest that she is aware of the possibility that the king may see her. However, as she chose to bathe *in the evening*, we do have an indicator that she may have wanted the privacy semidarkness provided. Simply put, "there is no indication in the text that the woman deliberately positioned herself so as to entice David." The narrator has no intention of casting Bathsheba as a temptress. . . . The indications that we have in the text, then, show Bathsheba to be a faithful woman minding her own business.[5]

Questions:

1. If you could live your life all over again and could do just one thing differently, what would it be?

2. If David could change one thing in his life, it would be his sin with Bathsheba. What can you learn from David's sins so that you will not allow the same destruction in your own life?

3. If you have made some of these same mistakes, or been the victim of other people's sins, what gives you hope about 2 Samuel 11 and 12?

Day Twenty-Three

Pictures of Grace

Sizing up a Cover-up

If we stay above reproach, we live below temptation.
Natalie Chambers Snapp[1]

Sin does not serve well as a gardener of the soul.
It landscapes the contour of the soul until all that is beautiful
has been made ugly; until all that is high is made low; until all
that is promising is wasted. Then life is like the desert
—parched and barren. It is drained of purpose.
It is bleached of happiness. Sin, then, is not wise,
but wasteful. It is not a gate, but only a grave.
C. Neil Strait, quoted in Lloyd Cory *Quote Unquote*[2]

Text: 2 Samuel 11:6-13
⁶ So David sent word to Joab, "Send me Uriah the Hittite."
And Joab sent Uriah to David. ⁷ When Uriah came to him, David
asked how Joab was doing and how the people were doing and
how the war was going. ⁸ Then David said to Uriah, "Go down to
your house and wash your feet." And Uriah went out of the king's
house, and there followed him a present from the king. ⁹ But
Uriah slept at the door of the king's house with all the servants
of his lord, and did not go down to his house.¹⁰ When they told
David, "Uriah did not go down to his house," David said to Uriah,
"Have you not come from a journey? Why did you not go down
to your house?" ¹¹ Uriah said to David, "The ark and Israel and
Judah dwell in booths, and my lord Joab and the servants of my
lord are camping in the open field. Shall I then go to my house, to

eat and to drink and to lie with my wife? As you live, and as your soul lives, I will not do this thing." ¹² Then David said to Uriah, "Remain here today also, and tomorrow I will send you back." So Uriah remained in Jerusalem that day and the next. ¹³ And David invited him, and he ate in his presence and drank, so that he made him drunk. And in the evening he went out to lie on his couch with the servants of his lord, but he did not go down to his house.

Thoughts:

These verses remind me of the words of warning found in Proverbs 28:13. "Whoever conceals his transgressions will not prosper, but he who confesses and forsakes them will obtain mercy." The NKJV reads, "He who covers his sins will not prosper, but whoever confesses and forsakes them will have mercy." This proverb has been referred to as "The Law of Revival." True revival occurs when we are walking with God in repentance, forgiveness, and restoration.

You will never find God's will when you are hiding your sin. In fact, hiding your sin leads to more sin. It is like digging the hole you fell in deeper and saying you are trying to get out. Just ask David how that played out for him. Rather than admitting his sin with Bathsheba and allowing God to forgive him and restore Bathsheba's marriage, David continued to sin. Concealing his sin led to him breaking more of God's commandments. Instead of fessing up, David tried to cover-up, and it ended messed-up!

Questions:

1. In what ways have you tried to hide your sins?

2. Why do you think you try to hide them in the first place?

3. How can you apply Proverbs 28:13 to your daily walk with the Lord so that you can find His mercy?

Day Twenty-Four

Pictures of Grace

Premeditated Sin

The first and worst of all fraud is to cheat oneself.
All sin is easy after that.
Philip Bailey, *nineteenth century poet*[1]

When we keep our pain in the dark,
we give the enemy the reins;
but when we surrender our pain to the light,
we give the reins to God.
Natalie Chambers Snapp[2]

Text: 2 Samuel 11:14-25

14 In the morning David wrote a letter to Joab and sent it by the hand of Uriah. **15** In the letter he wrote, "Set Uriah in the forefront of the hardest fighting, and then draw back from him, that he may be struck down, and die." **16** And as Joab was besieging the city, he assigned Uriah to the place where he knew there were valiant men. **17** And the men of the city came out and fought with Joab, and some of the servants of David among the people fell. Uriah the Hittite also died. **18** Then Joab sent and told David all the news about the fighting. **19** And he instructed the messenger, "When you have finished telling all the news about the fighting to the king, **20** then, if the king's anger rises, and if he says to you, 'Why did you go so near the city to fight? Did you not know that they would shoot from the wall? **21** Who killed Abimelech the son of Jerubbesheth? Did not a woman cast an upper millstone on him from the wall, so that he died at Thebez? Why did you go so near the wall?' then you shall say, 'Your servant Uriah the Hittite is dead also.'" 22 So the messenger went and came and told David all that Joab had sent him to tell. 23 The messenger said to David, "The men gained an advantage over us and came out against us in the field, but we drove them back to the entrance of the gate. 24 Then the archers shot at your servants from the wall. Some of the king's servants are dead, and your servant Uriah the Hittite is dead also." 25 David said to the messenger, "Thus shall you say to Joab, 'Do not let this matter displease you, for the sword devours now one and now another. Strengthen your attack against the city and overthrow it.' And encourage him."

Thoughts:

Please note the devastating effects of sin. It wasn't just Bathsheba who was hurt and victimized; Uriah would lose his life. In addition, other soldiers in David's army would die. Because of David's sin, a lot of innocent people were hurt. Don't ever think that your sin only hurts you. Every time we sin, innocent people are wounded. And it always breaks the heart of God.

Purposely hiding sin always leads to more sins. Sin that is kept secret manufactures guilt. Guilt and shame have an enormous effect on people. When we confess our sin, we find mercy. When we attempt to hide our sin, sin still has a hold on us. The longer we live in sin, the more impact our enemy has over our lives. Before you know it, what you tried to control by hiding your sin, is now controlling you. And once under the control of the devil, sinning becomes habitual.

Questions:

1. How do you deal with your guilt and shame over your secret sins?

2. How is praying in secret (Matthew 6:6, 18) a way to come clean before God?

3. In today's devotion, you read this statement: "Purposely hiding your sin always leads to more sins." Consider this statement and write down your thoughts.

Day Twenty-Five

Pictures of Grace

Finding Healing in our Hurt

Bathsheba's suffering led her to bear fruit that grew
while she was in the deepest valley of her life.
Natalie Snapp

If we view our pain and suffering with an eternal perspective,
our own brokenness can nourish our future souls and the souls
of others.
Natalie Snapp[1]

Text: 2 Samuel 11:26-27
[26] When the wife of Uriah heard that Uriah her husband
was dead, she lamented over her husband. [27] And when the
mourning was over, David sent and brought her to his house,
and she became his wife and bore him a son. But the thing that
David had done displeased the Lord.

Thoughts:
The Scripture is clear that David's sin displeased the Lord.
Notice it didn't say, "Bathsheba's sin." Nowhere does Scripture say
that Bathsheba sinned. We are not told one time that Bathsheba's
actions angered or displeased God. Bathsheba has been the
victim of David's inability to find victory over his temptations.

Natalie Snapp sums up Bathsheba's pain with these words:

So now Bathsheba had been forced to commit
adultery, was pregnant with an illegitimate child, and her

99

husband was dead. I'd say Bathsheba was experiencing some trauma, wouldn't you?[2]

In her insightful book, *The Bathsheba Battle: Finding Hope When Life Takes an Unexpected Turn,* Snapp gives these words concerning healing.

> Healing is a process; so, while some immediately feel set free from their pain, not everyone does. However, the first step of healing is to recognize you cannot carry your burdens alone anymore. I love the words of Matthew 11:28-30. I love how *The Message* summarizes these verses: "Are you tired? Worn out? Burned out on religion? Come to me. Get away with me and you'll recover your life. I'll show you how to take a real rest. Walk with me and work with me; watch how I do it. Learn the unforced rhythms of grace. I won't lay anything heavy or ill-fitting on you. Keep company with me and you'll learn to live freely and lightly." Living freely and lightly sounds wonderful, doesn't it?
>
> All our pain and suffering, which is our trauma, affects our lives. Healing this trauma certainly isn't easy; however, the reward for having the courage to start the process of healing from your trauma has the power to change the complete trajectory of your family line.[3]

Bathsheba found healing and a restored life. Both Bathsheba and David found healing and restoration. Their examples in Scripture give us hope that God can heal and restore us as well.

Questions:

1. Explain your reactions to the two quotes by Natalie Snapp that begin today's devotion.

2. Hurt people usually hurt people. How can you change your response to pain and bring more healing instead of more hurt?

3. How can you apply Matthew 11:28-30 to your life?

Pictures of Grace

A Strategy for Grace

"God does not allow His children to sin successfully."
Charles Spurgeon[1]

The greater the man, the dearer price he pays
for a short season of sinful pleasure.
F. B. Meyer, *David*[2]

To be the man after God's own heart
is not to be sinlessly perfect but to be, among other things,
utterly submissive to the accusing word of God.
Dale Ralph Davis[3]

Text: 2 Samuel 12:1-15a

[1] And the Lord sent Nathan to David. He came to him and said to him, "There were two men in a certain city, the one rich and the other poor. [2] The rich man had very many flocks and herds, [3] but the poor man had nothing but one little ewe lamb, which he had bought. And he brought it up, and it grew up with him and with his children. It used to eat of his morsel and drink from his cup and lie in his arms, and it was like a daughter to him. [4] Now there came a traveler to the rich man, and he was unwilling to take one of his own flock or herd to prepare for the guest who had come to him, but he took the poor man's lamb and prepared it for the man who had come to him." [5] Then David's anger was greatly kindled against the man, and he said to Nathan, "As the Lord lives, the man

who has done this deserves to die, [6] and he shall restore the lamb fourfold, because he did this thing, and because he had no pity."

[7] Nathan said to David, "You are the man! Thus says the Lord, the God of Israel, 'I anointed you king over Israel, and I delivered you out of the hand of Saul. [8] And I gave you your master's house and your master's wives into your arms and gave you the house of Israel and of Judah. And if this were too little, I would add to you as much more. [9] Why have you despised the word of the Lord, to do what is evil in his sight? You have struck down Uriah the Hittite with the sword and have taken his wife to be your wife and have killed him with the sword of the Ammonites. [10] Now therefore the sword shall never depart from your house, because you have despised me and have taken the wife of Uriah the Hittite to be your wife.' [11] Thus says the Lord, 'Behold, I will raise up evil against you out of your own house. And I will take your wives before your eyes and give them to your neighbor, and he shall lie with your wives in the sight of this sun. [12] For you did it secretly, but I will do this thing before all Israel and before the sun.'" [13] David said to Nathan, "I have sinned against the Lord." And Nathan said to David, "The Lord also has put away your sin; you shall not die. [14] Nevertheless, because by this deed you have utterly scorned the Lord, the child who is born to you shall die." [15] Then Nathan went to his house.

Thoughts:

Throughout the New Testament, Jesus taught through parables which brought great clarity to His teachings. Jesus is the Master storyteller, greatest Teacher, and King of all kings. In today's text, God gave a parable to His prophet Nathan for His earthly king, David. It is one of the best-known teaching parables in the Old Testament. And while there is nothing funny about this story whatsoever, this parable has possibly the greatest punchline in all of Scripture—"You are the man!"

God used an ingenious plan to get David's attention.

> Just because Nathan's a prophet doesn't mean he can't be sharp. But it's more than Nathan. Nathan's strategy is nothing but the ingenuity of grace. His technique is the godly scheming of grace that goes around the end of our resistance and causes us to switch the floodlights on our own darkness. Some of you may need to repent—you've thought all these years that only the Serpent was subtle (Genesis 3:1)![4]

God used craftiness in both the storyline and the strategy behind telling it. Sometimes, we only acknowledge our own sin when we are unknowingly confronted with it through the story of somebody's life. Our sinful nature has a way of tricking us into pointing out the sins of others while ignoring our own sins.

The symbolism throughout this parable is unique.

> The "traveler" whom the rich man fed represents the temptation and lust that visited David on the roof and then controlled him. If we open the door, sin comes in as a guest but soon becomes the master. (Genesis 4:6—7).
>
> David passed judgment on the rich man without realizing he was passing judgment on himself. Of all blindness, the worst kind is that which makes us blind to ourselves.[5]

2 Samuel 12:5 reveals that David responded to the story with great anger. It fired David up that someone would sin with such disregard to how it hurt others. Warren Wiersbe adds:

If David, a mere mortal sinner, has the moral capacity to fly into a rage over Nathan's rich man (vs. 5—6), how much more will Yahweh over David's deed? So He should. This is the gracious God who sends Nathan to David, and He is the furious God who is outraged because his servant has despised Him. Part of God's grace consists in His informing us of His fury. Sometimes we try to de-claw grace. But grace is not niceness; otherwise (one is tempted to say), grace would no longer be grace. We forget the words of the hymn: "Twas grace that *taught my heart to fear....*' Grace is not merely favor; it is also the fury that precedes the favor.[6]

Even through all of David's disobedience and deceit, God still showed His grace. When David confessed, God responded. Nathan told David in verse 13, "The Lord also has put away your sin; ..."

Only when we understand the reality and seriousness of sin are we ready to wonder at God's grace. He "put away" David's sin (v. 13). David's sin did not do all the damage that it could have done, but only because God was gracious. It did not destroy God's good purposes. And for that reason, we are privileged to know the Son of David, who was named Jesus, "for He will save his people from their sins" (Matthew 1:21).[7]

Questions:

1. We may deceive ourselves about our evil thoughts, words, and deeds. But evil cannot be hidden from God! Why is it so hard for you to confess your sins to a God who already knows?

2. How can envisioning the consequences help motivate you to say no to temptation?

3. What are your thoughts on the following statement from today's devotion? "Sometimes, we only acknowledge our own sin when we are unknowingly confronted with it through the story of somebody's life."

Day Twenty-Seven

Pictures of Grace

Consequences of Sin

When we diffuse fear, we infuse hope.
Natalie Chambers Snapp[1]

The man who for too long had acted only in self-interest
at last cared about someone else:
he sought God "on behalf of the child."
John Woodhouse[2]

If a man gets drunk and goes out and breaks his leg so that it
must be amputated, God will forgive him if he asks it, but he will
still have to hop around on one leg all his life.
Dwight L. Moody (1837-1899), evangelist[3]

Text: 2 Samuel 12:15b-23

[15] . . . And the Lord afflicted the child that Uriah's wife bore to David, and he became sick. [16] David therefore sought God on behalf of the child. And David fasted and went in and lay all night on the ground. [17] And the elders of his house stood beside him, to raise him from the ground, but he would not, nor did he eat food with them. [18] On the seventh day the child died. And the servants of David were afraid to tell him that the child was dead, for they said, "Behold, while the child was yet alive, we spoke to him, and he did not listen to us. How then can we say to him the child is dead? He may do himself some harm." [19] But when David saw that his servants were whispering together, David understood that the child was dead. And David said to his servants, "Is the

child dead?" They said, "He is dead." **²⁰** Then David arose from the earth and washed and anointed himself and changed his clothes. And he went into the house of the Lord and worshiped. He then went to his own house. And when he asked, they set food before him, and he ate. **²¹** Then his servants said to him, "What is this thing that you have done? You fasted and wept for the child while he was alive; but when the child died, you arose and ate food." **²²** He said, "While the child was still alive, I fasted and wept, for I said, 'Who knows whether the Lord will be gracious to me, that the child may live?' **²³** But now he is dead. Why should I fast? Can I bring him back again? I shall go to him, but he will not return to me."

Thoughts:

God is both a forgiving and just God. While God offers forgiveness for sins, there are still consequences for falling short of the glory of God.

> The doctrines of sin and redemption can be complicated—for non-Christians, of course, but also for many Christians. One problem nearly every pastor can attest to encountering is the confusion of sin's *punishment* and its *consequences*. When sin creates a rift in our lives, the response is often bewilderment. *Hasn't Jesus conquered sin?* we think. *Why is this still so damaging?* What we are struggling with in those moments is distinguishing the punishment for our sin from the natural consequences of it. And while Jesus absorbs sin's punishments, He does not always remove every consequence.[4]

Scripture clearly says, "… the Lord afflicted the child…" This is a hard subject for most people. May the words of Dale Ralph Davis give us clarity.

Yahweh forgives the guilt of sin but inflicts the consequences of sin. He cleanses sin's defilement but may continue its discipline. For David, Yahweh's forgiveness was both marvelous and costly—the child would die. It is as if the child will die in David's place. There was no doubt that David was the one under the threat of death. David himself had judged Nathan's rich man a 'son of death' (v. 5). Yet Nathan had assured David that he would not die (v. 13). But a death would occur. The child to be born would die (v. 14b). It is as if the child is David's substitute. I do not intend to read New Testament meanings back into an Old Testament text. I only want readers to note the pattern here, for there are some of us who know this paradox of forgiveness that is both free and costly, because a son of David has been our substitute.[5]

David's response to his child's sickness reveals his faith in God.

David thought that maybe Yahweh's sentence (v. 14b) was not his last word. Maybe, David thought, he's stirring me to pray. It all rests on David's thinking, his assumption, about God. 'I thought, "Who knows? Yahweh may show grace to me!"' See how well David knows his God! Showing grace is Yahweh's forte. And who can tell what a God like that may delight to do in this case? Who can imagine how gracious a God of all grace wants to be to us in our sins and messes? For David, grace is not a doctrinal concept but the peculiar bent of God's nature.[6]

David's response to the child's death is perplexing. John Woodhouse's commentary provides a great explanation.

> It is important to notice that David's prayer for his child did not involve knowing what God would do. He prayed because God had been gracious to him, but not because he knew in this particular matter whether God would or would not grant his request.
> After the death of the child, God's will was known. David knew that his prayers would not now bring the child back. David understood the finality of death. The possibility that had led him to pray was now gone. The time would come when David would die, as his son had now died. But the child who had died would not return to his father.
> David's quiet acceptance of the death of his child suggests contentment with God's wisdom and trust in his goodness. He was a remarkably changed man![7]

God's grace and sin's consequences both have a way of restoring and transforming our lives. If sin had no consequence and only forgiveness, people would abuse God's grace. If sin had no forgiveness and only consequences, our efforts at goodness would only be for selfish reasons. However, God's forgiveness and His grace stir our hearts to love Him more. Consequences keep our minds alert to learn from our mistakes so that we will not repeat them. One produces love, the other promotes learning.

Questions:

1. How does God's forgiveness and sins' consequences motivate you towards a life of righteousness?

2. How can we respond with worship even while still in pain? Be specific.

3. How has God's grace and sin's consequences combined to transform your life?

Day Twenty-Eight

Pictures of Grace

The God who Names

We are most like beasts when we kill. We are most like men
when we judge. We are most like God when we forgive.
William Arthur Ward, *Thoughts of a Christian Optimist*[1]

Forgiveness is surrendering my right
to hurt you for hurting me.
Archibald Hart, **in James Dobson, *Love Must Be Tough*[2]**

Text: 2 Samuel 12:24-25
[24] Then David comforted his wife, Bathsheba, and went in to
her and lay with her, and she bore a son, and he called his name
Solomon. And the Lord loved him [25] and sent a message by
Nathan the prophet. So he called his name Jedidiah, because
of the Lord.

Thoughts:
A lot can be learned through Scripture by looking at names.
The characteristics of Jesus can also be linked to how He names
His children. God's sovereignty, salvation, redemption, and
restoration can all be discovered by looking at the meaning
behind the names.

Showering his mercy upon them, God gave David
and Bathsheba a second son (vv. 24—25). The couple
named the child Solomon, which means "peace,
peaceful, restoration." By naming the child Solomon,

David was declaring that the LORD had now given him and Bathsheba peace. Note that the LORD loved Solomon, an indication that the LORD was setting him apart for a very special service. Because of the LORD's special love, he sent word through Nathan the prophet that the child was to be given a second name, that of Jedidiah, which means "beloved of the LORD." This child was to have a very special ministry in the future, replacing David as the anointed king of Israel. Solomon will be the appointed person to build the temple of the LORD.[3]

Jesus, the Name above all names has a special way of naming His own.

The world doesn't show forgiveness, nor does it extend grace. The world labels people by their sins. No one names their children after some of these ladies listed in the genealogy of Jesus. I have known many women named Ruth, but have never met a Tamar, Rahab, or Bathsheba. I wonder if it is because we associate those three names with great sin, whereas the Bible associates them with great grace. And as we have seen in Bathsheba's case, she gets a bad reputation from most, when she was the one hurt by the sin of David. I am so thankful that we have a God who judges sin while at the same time extends grace. The world will never love us nor extend grace to us like Jesus. While the world may never know our name or even care to, Jesus knows us by name and loves us.

Questions:

1. Today, you read this statement by Archibald Hart: "Forgiveness is surrendering my right to hurt you for hurting me." Write down your thoughts on this statement.

2. Imagine how much joy and healing it brought Bathsheba and David each time they called their son's name. What do you think God feels each time He calls you by name?

3. How can you live in such a way to bring honor to His name?

Day Twenty-Nine

Pictures of Grace

A Christmas List of Grace

The spirit of Christmas needs to be superseded by the Spirit
of Christ. The spirit of Christmas is annual; the Spirit of Christ
is eternal. The spirit of Christmas is sentimental; the Spirit
of Christ is supernatural. The spirit of Christmas is a human
product; the Spirit of Christ is a divine person.
That makes all the difference in the world.
Stuart Briscoe, *Meet Him at the Manger, Christianity Today*

In Jesus we now rightly understand the beginning
because we can now see the end. . .
It is the Christian conviction, a conviction shaped by the
grammar of the first verse of the gospel of Matthew,
that we can know there was a beginning,
because we have seen the end in the
life, death, and resurrection of Jesus Christ.
Stanley Hauerwas[1]

Text: Matthew 1:1, 16-17
[1] The book of the genealogy of Jesus Christ, the son of David, the son of Abraham. . . [16] and Jacob the father of Joseph the
husband of Mary, of whom Jesus was born, who is called Christ.
[17] So all the generations from Abraham to David were fourteen
generations, and from David to the deportation to Babylon fourteen generations, and from the deportation to Babylon to the
Christ fourteen generations.

Thoughts:

Merry Christmas! As you have studied the lives of Tamar, Rahab, Ruth, and Bathsheba, you have witnessed picture after picture of God's amazing grace. Now we come to the earthly mother of our heavenly Savior—Mary, the mother of Jesus. Over the next week, we will study Mary's relationship with Jesus and learn more about our own walk with the Lord. But it's Christmas, so let's focus on just a few verses from Matthew's first chapter and marvel at this list of grace found in the genealogy of Jesus.

One commentary expressed grace in Jesus' genealogy with these words:

> God saves only by His sovereign grace. The list of names in verses 1—17 is full of evil kings and sinful men and women, a description that includes Abraham and David as well. Abraham was a polygamist patriarch who lied about his wife twice. David was an adulterous murderer. And the list goes on and on. It's amazing to think that the great, great, great, great, great grandparents of Jesus hated God and were leading other people to hate Him too. Clearly, then, Jesus came not because of Israel's righteousness, but in spite of Israel's sinfulness.[2]

God works in spite of our sins, and unconditionally blesses us with His grace. Therefore, we see grace all over His genealogy.

We also discover that the goal of this genealogy is to point us to the end of the list, to Jesus—the Lord of grace!

> As though to emphasize that Jesus isn't just one member in an ongoing family, but the actual goal of the whole list, he arranges the genealogy into three groups of 14 names—or, perhaps we should say, into six groups of seven names. The number seven was and

116

is one of the most powerful symbolic numbers, and to be born at the beginning of the seventh seven in the sequence is clearly to be the climax of the whole list.

This birth, Matthew is saying, is what Israel has been waiting for these past two thousand years.[3]

This imperfect list of people points us to the Lord of all. This genealogy filled with people who have all sinned leads us to the Lord who has come to save. Matthew begins his Gospel with a gallery of pictures that all have one message—grace! Each picture points to one person—The Messiah. The first fifteen verses of Matthew have been a drumroll that leads to the declaration of the birth of Jesus.

During this season of Christmas, take some time to open God's photo album of grace and walk down memory lane. As you turn page after page of people God has blessed, remember the times He has showered you with His grace. Look at the life of Abraham. God told him to leave everything he knew and take his family to a place he had never been. Abraham's faith grew with each part of the journey. He made mistakes all along the way. However, God's grace was right with him every step of the way. Consider David, known as the man after God's own heart. Yet, David made countless mistakes and sinned greatly. However, not one sin was greater than God's grace. God still used David mightily for His purposes because of His grace. In the middle of this list, you will come to a man named Jehoshaphat (vs. 8). If you studied 2 Chronicles 20, you would know that he faced an impossible situation. He had no idea what to do, but he kept his eyes on the Lord. He gave His mess to the Lord and witnessed a God-sized miracle.

The list of God's grace and goodness is unending. As you think about all that God has done; may it give you great confidence in what He can still do. If you are believer, you've been grafted into His family tree. You are in His family because of your faith. This also places you in the genealogy of His grace. Praying you have a grace-filled Christmas!

Questions:

1. In his commentary on Matthew, Stanley Hauerwas does an excellent job explaining why Matthew wrote his Gospel.

> Matthew wrote his Gospel to position the reader to be a follower of Jesus. Matthew wrote knowing what he and many of his readers knew, that Jesus would be killed and raised from the dead. The problem was that such knowledge did his readers no good unless they were trained in the same manner that Jesus had trained his own disciples: to be a follower of Jesus through the reading of the gospel. Matthew understands that most of us will be tempted to be a member of the ever-present crowd depicted in the gospel. The crowd was often impressed by Jesus' teachings and his miracles, but when push came to shove, the crowd called for his crucifixion. Jesus's disciples also abandoned him at the end, but Jesus had called them to follow him, making them the continuation of the story. Matthew rightly hopes that through the reading of the gospel we may be no less.[4]

After reading these words, where do you see yourself in your walk with Jesus?

2. Are you part of the crowd around Jesus?
   Or are you a committed follower of Jesus Christ?

3. What is God currently doing in your life that is new?

Day Thirty

Pictures of Grace

Grace in Place of Disgrace

It was the story of Jesus' birth told by early Christians that led to the reading of Isaiah 7:14 in a new light, not the other way around. If we ask the significance of the virgin conception, it stresses: (1) the holiness of the child, for He was conceived through the agency of the Holy Spirit; (2) the uniqueness of the child, for such means of conception is unprecedented; (3) the divinity of the child because by this means it was made clear He was the Son of God.
Ben Witherington III[1]

Text: Matthew 1:18-25
[18] Now the birth of Jesus Christ took place in this way. When his mother Mary had been betrothed to Joseph, before they came together she was found to be with child from the Holy Spirit. [19] And her husband Joseph, being a just man and unwilling to put her to shame, resolved to divorce her quietly. [20] But as he considered these things, behold, an angel of the Lord appeared to him in a dream, saying, "Joseph, son of David, do not fear to take Mary as your wife, for that which is conceived in her is from the Holy Spirit. [21] She will bear a son, and you shall call his name Jesus, for he will save his people from their sins." [22] All this took place to fulfill what the Lord had spoken by the prophet: [23] "Behold, the virgin shall conceive and bear a son, and they shall call his name Immanuel" (which means, God with us). [24] When Joseph woke from sleep, he did as the angel of the Lord commanded him: he took his

wife, ²⁵ but knew her not until she had given birth to a son. And he called his name Jesus.

Thoughts:

The biblical account of the birth of Jesus is full of practical insights that need to be applied to our spiritual journey.

The word usually translated *birth* in verse 18 is the same Greek word *genesis* that Matthew used in verse 1, where it is translated *genealogy*. By repeating this word, Matthew connects this new paragraph with the genealogy and reemphasizes the new creation theme by which he understands Jesus.[2]

In the use of that one word, God reinforces the truth that Jesus has come to make all things new. His virgin birth, sinless life, sacrificial death, and powerful resurrection made possible a new birth and new life spiritually for everyone who accepts His grace by faith! He who knew no sin became sin so that we could become the righteousness of God. (2 Corinthians 5:21). Jesus came so that we could exchange our disgrace for His grace!

Mary and Joseph experienced this exchange in their own journey with Jesus. Most people don't understand the scandal that surrounded Mary and Joseph when it became known that she was pregnant. The following commentary might bring some clarity.

To understand this one must recognize that in Jewish marriage there were three steps. The first step was the engagement, a contract arranged by family members who determined whether the couple would be well suited for each other and for a future marriage. Second, there was the betrothal, the public ratification of the engagement, with a period of one year for the couple to become known as belonging to each other, but not having the rights of living together as husband and wife. The only way a betrothal could be terminated was by a divorce. In Jewish law there is a phrase which states that a young woman whose fiancé dies during the period of betrothal is called "a virgin who is a widow." Mary and Joseph were in the second stage in the account of this text. The third stage is the marriage proper, which took place at the end of the year of betrothal.

It was during the year of their betrothal that Mary made known to Joseph that she was with child by the miraculous act of God. Joseph is referred to as a just man with special love and consideration for Mary. Confronted with the problem of his betrothed being pregnant, he contemplated how to end the betrothal in a divorce. He sought ways to do it privately rather than to expose her publicly.

Mary was pledged and pregnant, and Joseph knew that the child was not his own. Mary's apparent unfaithfulness carried a severe social stigma. According to Jewish civil law, Joseph had the right to divorce her. The law also explained that the penalty for unchastity was death by stoning (Deuteronomy 22:23—24), although this was rarely carried out at this time.[3]

Therefore, Mary and Joseph were subject to public disgrace because Mary was pregnant. Mary and Joseph had one thing in common with Tamar, Rahab, Ruth, and Bathsheba. The world looked at all of them with judgmental eyes of disgrace. But Jesus loved them all through His unconditional grace.

As we are headed to a new year with Jesus, there are wonderful truths here to apply to our daily lives. No one needs to be reminded that we live in a world that is extremely judgmental. People do a great job spreading rumors, gossip, and bad news; but for some reason have a difficult time sharing the Good News of Jesus. The world gives up on most people when they make mistakes. Yet, God takes our mistakes and turns them into pictures of His grace.

This reminds me of Romans 8:28 where Paul says, "... we know that for those who love God all things work together for good, for those who are called according to His purpose." God has a plan for His people and can take even our mess-ups and turn them into His masterpieces. As we enter a new year, make sure to remember that our God is making everything new. We all sin and fall short of the glory of God. We all need forgiveness. Thank God that He forgives and gives second chances.

Questions:

1. Are you quick to judge others while you want God to be patient with you? Why?

2. Are you slow to forgive others while you want God to quickly forgive you? Why?

3. Why do you think people want God's goodness for their lives but want His judgment for others? What does this say about our concept of God and our concern for others?

4. Where in your life has God given you grace in place of disgrace?

5. Who in your life needs to see His grace through your love?

Day Thirty-One

Pictures of Grace

Never Alone

Many Christmas celebrations miss the enormity of Christ's
birth. This was not just another baby or another birthday.
God was born in human likeness—the Divine taking upon
himself the limitations of humanity. This event is understood
by us to be the *incarnation*. The mystery of the incarnation
should always override our tendency to turn Jesus into a
cuddly baby we can handle and control. He is Emmanuel—God
with us—wrapped in human flesh (Isa. 7:14; Matt. 1:23).
It is hard to wrap our minds around it, but it is true.
He became flesh and dwelled among us (John 1:14).
He was made like us so we could be made like Him.
Ken Heer[1]

Text: Luke 2:1-7
[1] In those days a decree went out from Caesar Augustus
that all the world should be registered. [2] This was the first
registration when Quirinius was governor of Syria. [3] And all
went to be registered, each to his own town. [4] And Joseph also
went up from Galilee, from the town of Nazareth, to Judea,
to the city of David, which is called Bethlehem, because he was
of the house and lineage of David, [5] to be registered with Mary,
his betrothed, who was with child. [6] And while they were there,
the time came for her to give birth. [7] And she gave birth to her
firstborn son and wrapped him in swaddling cloths and laid him
in a manger, because there was no place for them in the inn.

Thoughts:

The seasons of Christmas and a New Year can be a difficult time for many people. In a world filled with social media connections, many people still live isolated lives. There has never been a better time for people to find true biblical fellowship and community. We were all created with a deep longing to belong!

I am reminded that Mary and Joseph found themselves alone during the first Christmas. It was difficult enough to deal with public disgrace but add to that being physically distanced from your family and friends.

> Caesar's decree denied her the support of family and friends, forcing her and Joseph to instead embark on an 85-mile journey from Nazareth to Bethlehem. The crowds clogging all the available housing eliminated the opportunity for even a traditional delivery; finding nowhere else to spend the night, Mary gave birth in a stable and laid her child in a manger (Luke 2:4—7). Rather than being congratulated by throngs of familiar faces, Mary and Joseph were visited by local shepherds—strangers—who had learned of the newborn Messiah from a startling encounter with the heavenly host.[2]

Even though Mary and Joseph were away from their home, God blessed them with new relationships. Worship has a way of bringing strangers together. You are never alone because of His presence. In addition, the joy of experiencing Jesus brings us closer to others.

Questions:

1. How does the worldly culture of Christmas distract you from the true worship of Christ?

2. How does your worship of Jesus bring you the joy of His presence?

3. How can worshiping Him genuinely help you experience biblical community?

Day Thirty-Two

Pictures of Grace

The Value of His Favor

The hinge of history is on the door of a Bethlehem stable.
Ralph W. Sockman [1]

Text: Luke 2:8-20

⁸ And in the same region there were shepherds out in the field, keeping watch over their flock by night. ⁹ And an angel of the Lord appeared to them, and the glory of the Lord shone around them, and they were filled with great fear. ¹⁰ And the angel said to them, "Fear not, for behold, I bring you good news of great joy that will be for all the people. ¹¹ For unto you is born this day in the city of David a Savior, who is Christ the Lord. ¹² And this will be a sign for you: you will find a baby wrapped in swaddling cloths and lying in a manger." ¹³ And suddenly there was with the angel a multitude of the heavenly host praising God and saying, ¹⁴ "Glory to God in the highest, and on earth peace among those with whom he is pleased!" ¹⁵ When the angels went away from them into heaven, the shepherds said to one another, "Let us go over to Bethlehem and see this thing that has happened, which the Lord has made known to us." ¹⁶ And they went with haste and found Mary and Joseph, and the baby lying in a manger.¹⁷ And when they saw it, they made known the saying that had been told them concerning this child. ¹⁸ And all who heard it wondered at what the shepherds told them. ¹⁹ But Mary treasured up all these things, pondering them in her heart. ²⁰ And the shepherds returned, glorifying and praising God for all they had heard and seen, as it had been told them.

Thoughts:

Both Matthew and Luke tell how the extraordinary story of Jesus is revealed to ordinary lives. I love the fact that God sent His angel to shepherds. While the leaders of Jesus' day missed Him, the lowly shepherds found Him. God is the same yesterday, today, and forever. This means that He still comes to those the world shuns. God has a unique way of showing His favor to those forgotten by the world. Perhaps God does it this way because certain people understand and appreciate the value of His favor.

Mary understood the magnitude of the moment God had blessed her with. She appreciated the worth of this encounter with Jesus.

Mary treasured all these words and pondered them in her heart. "Treasured" means deep reflection, keeping in mind or safely storing up; "pondering in the heart" refers to mulling over, seeking to understand and interpret. Mary had a lot to think about as she gazed into the face of her tiny child. Gabriel had told her that the little boy would reign forever (1:31—33); the shepherds reported the angel's words—He is the Savior, Christ the Lord (2:11). As Mary held this tiny baby, she must have wondered at all that God was doing, and who her son would grow up to become.[2]

Questions:

1. Christmas season comes and goes every year. However, every day we have opportunities to encounter Jesus. If we are not focused on Christ, we could easily miss out on all that He has for us. How do you treasure your time with Jesus? In what ways, can you miss the magnitude of your personal moments with Him?

2. In what specific ways can you trust God to take the ordinary parts of your day and make them extraordinary for His glory?

Day Thirty-Three

Pictures of Grace

Seeking Salvation

You will seek Me and find Me,
when you seek Me with all your heart.
Jeremiah 29:13

Text: Luke 2:21-38

21 And at the end of eight days, when he was circumcised, he was called Jesus, the name given by the angel before he was conceived in the womb. 22 And when the time came for their purification according to the Law of Moses, they brought him up to Jerusalem to present him to the Lord 23 (as it is written in the Law of the Lord, "Every male who first opens the womb shall be called holy to the Lord") 24 and to offer a sacrifice according to what is said in the Law of the Lord, "a pair of turtledoves, or two young pigeons." 25 Now there was a man in Jerusalem, whose name was Simeon, and this man was righteous and devout, waiting for the consolation of Israel, and the Holy Spirit was upon him. 26 And it had been revealed to him by the Holy Spirit that he would not see death before he had seen the Lord's Christ. 27 And he came in the Spirit into the temple, and when the parents brought in the child Jesus, to do for him according to the custom of the Law, 28 he took him up in his arms and blessed God and said, 29 "Lord, now you are letting your servant depart in peace, according to your word; 30 for my eyes have seen your salvation 31 that you have prepared in the presence of all peoples, 32 a light for revelation to the Gentiles, and for glory to your people Israel." 33 And his father and his

mother marveled at what was said about him. **³⁴** And Simeon blessed them and said to Mary his mother, "Behold, this child is appointed for the fall and rising of many in Israel, and for a sign that is opposed **³⁵** (and a sword will pierce through your own soul also), so that thoughts from many hearts may be revealed." **³⁶** And there was a prophetess, Anna, the daughter of Phanuel, of the tribe of Asher. She was advanced in years, having lived with her husband seven years from when she was a virgin, **³⁷** and then as a widow until she was eighty-four. She did not depart from the temple, worshiping with fasting and prayer night and day. **³⁸** And coming up at that very hour she began to give thanks to God and to speak of him to all who were waiting for the redemption of Jerusalem.

Thoughts:

Imagine waiting on something extremely important and being promised you would see it before you die. Simeon was a righteous and devout man and the Holy Spirit revealed to him that he would not die before he had personally seen the Messiah. I wonder what that must have been like for Simeon. I envision that Simeon looked for Jesus every day of his life. That would be a great lesson for all of us—looking for Jesus every single day. Please note that the Spirit led Simeon to the temple the day he met Jesus. The Spirit always leads us to find Jesus. May the Spirit daily lead you to Jesus as you seek the Lord passionately.

Questions:

1. Have you come to the point in your life where you have trusted Jesus Christ as your Lord and Savior? Are you a Christian?

2. If so, describe what it was like when your eyes personally saw the salvation of the Lord.

3. Are you seeking Jesus daily? If so, how? If not, why?

Day Thirty-Four

Pictures of Grace

Falling Down to Worship Him

Worship is a meeting between God and His people
when the worshiper is brought into personal contact
with the one who gives meaning and purpose to life;
from this encounter the worshiper receives strength
and courage to live with hope in a fallen world.
Robert Webber[1]

If worship is just one thing we do,
Everything becomes mundane.
If worship is the one thing we do,
everything takes on eternal significance.
Timothy J. Christenson

Worship does not satisfy our hunger for God;
it whets our appetite.
Eugene H. Peterson[2]

Text: Matthew 2:1-12
   [1] Now after Jesus was born in Bethlehem of Judea in the days of Herod the king, behold, wise men from the east came to Jerusalem, [2] saying, "Where is he who has been born king of the Jews? For we saw his star when it rose and have come to worship him." [3] When Herod the king heard this, he was troubled, and all Jerusalem with him; [4] and assembling all the chief priests and scribes of the people, he inquired of them where the Christ was to be born. [5] They told him, "In Bethlehem of Judea, for so it is

written by the prophet: ⁶ "'And you, O Bethlehem, in the land of Judah, are by no means least among the rulers of Judah; for from you shall come a ruler who will shepherd my people Israel.'" ⁷ Then Herod summoned the wise men secretly and ascertained from them what time the star had appeared. ⁸ And he sent them to Bethlehem, saying, "Go and search diligently for the child, and when you have found him, bring me word, that I too may come and worship him." ⁹ After listening to the king, they went on their way. And behold, the star that they had seen when it rose went before them until it came to rest over the place where the child was. ¹⁰ When they saw the star, they rejoiced exceedingly with great joy. ¹¹ And going into the house, they saw the child with Mary his mother, and they fell down and worshiped him. Then, opening their treasures, they offered him gifts, gold and frankincense and myrrh. ¹² And being warned in a dream not to return to Herod, they departed to their own country by another way.

Thoughts:

In recent years, there has been more clarity regarding the wise men who came to worship Jesus. For years, nativity scenes depicted wise men around the birth of Jesus. Now, some people are removing the wise men and putting them somewhere else in the house to symbolize the fact that they didn't arrive until sometime later. Here is how Bruce Barton explains it in his commentary on Matthew.

Most scholars believe that the traditional nonbiblical picture of the wise men arriving at the manger is incorrect based on clues given in this chapter. More likely, the wise men arrived some time after Jesus' birth—Jesus is called a child (*paidion,* 2:9, 11) rather than a baby or infant (*brephos,* used in Luke 2:12), and the wise men went to a house (2:11), not to a stable. The fact that Herod had all the baby boys under two years old killed (2:16) may mean that a couple of years had passed between Jesus' birth and this visit. If so, apparently Mary and Joseph decided to remain for a time in Bethlehem instead of returning after the census taking (Luke 2:1—5) to Nazareth.[3]

No matter what time they got there, these men worshiped Jesus. Verse 11 states that "they fell down and worshiped Him." The New Testament word "fell down" here means, "to descend from a standing position to a prostrate position." The word for "worship" here means "to kiss the ground." The Greek language of the New Testament uses two words here to double emphasize the fact that these wise men got on their faces before the Lord. Make no mistake, their wonder and awe of who Jesus was led them to humble themselves before Him and fall to the ground in worship.

Ronald Allen gives this profound discussion on worship in his book, *Worship: Rediscovering the Missing Jewel.*

What, then, is the essence of worship? It is the celebration of God! When we worship God, we celebrate Him: We extol Him, we sound His praises, we boast in Him.

Worship is not the casual chatter that occasionally drowns out the organ prelude; we celebrate God when we allow the prelude to attune our hearts to the glory of God by the means of the music.

Worship is not the mumbling of prayers or the mouthing of hymns with little thought and less heart; we celebrate God when we join together earnestly in prayer and intensely in song.

Worship is not self-aggrandizing words or boring clichés when one is asked to give a testimony; we celebrate

God when all of the parts of the service fit together and work to a common end.

Worship is not grudging gifts or compulsory service; we celebrate God when we give to Him hilariously and serve Him with integrity.

Worship is not haphazard music done poorly, not even great music done merely as a performance; we celebrate God when we enjoy and participate in music to His glory.

Worship is not a distracted endurance of the sermon; we celebrate God as we hear His Word gladly and seek to be conformed by it more and more to the image of our Savior.

Worship is not the hurried motions of a "tacked-on" Lord's Table; we celebrate God preeminently when we fellowship gratefully at the ceremonial meal that speaks so centrally of our faith in Christ Who died for us, Who rose again on our behalf, and Who is to return for our good.

As a thoughtful gift is a celebration of a birthday, as a special evening out is a celebration of an anniversary, as a warm eulogy is a celebration of a life, as a meaningful embrace is a celebration of a marriage—so a worship service is a celebration of God.[4]

Questions:

1. Does your wonder lead to worship?

2. When is the last time you have been on your face before the Lord in worship? How does going facedown put you in a proper position and attitude to approach Jesus?

3. Do you go to church to worship, or do you bring your worship to church? What is the difference between the two?

Day Thirty-Five

Pictures of Grace

Your Place in His Grace

Grace means there is nothing we can do to make God love us
more. . . And grace means there is nothing we can do to make
God love us less. . . Grace means that God already loves us as
much as an infinite God can possibly love.
Phillip Yancey, *What's so Amazing about Grace?*[1]

Text: Matthew 2:13-23

[13] Now when they had departed, behold, an angel of the
Lord appeared to Joseph in a dream and said, "Rise, take the
child and his mother, and flee to Egypt, and remain there until
I tell you, for Herod is about to search for the child, to destroy
him." [14] And he rose and took the child and his mother by night
and departed to Egypt [15] and remained there until the death
of Herod. This was to fulfill what the Lord had spoken by the
prophet, "Out of Egypt I called my son." [16] Then Herod, when he
saw that he had been tricked by the wise men, became furious,
and he sent and killed all the male children in Bethlehem and
in all that region who were two years old or under, according to
the time that he had ascertained from the wise men. [17] Then was
fulfilled what was spoken by the prophet Jeremiah: [18] "A voice
was heard in Ramah, weeping and loud lamentation, Rachel
weeping for her children; she refused to be comforted, because
they are no more." [19] But when Herod died, behold, an angel
of the Lord appeared in a dream to Joseph in Egypt, [20] saying,
"Rise, take the child and his mother and go to the land of Israel,
for those who sought the child's life are dead." [21] And he rose

and took the child and his mother and went to the land of Israel. ²²But when he heard that Archelaus was reigning over Judea in place of his father Herod, he was afraid to go there, and being warned in a dream he withdrew to the district of Galilee. ²³And he went and lived in a city called Nazareth, so that what was spoken by the prophets might be fulfilled, that he would be called a Nazarene.

Thoughts:

Three different prophecies are fulfilled in today's text. Matthew 2:15 notes one from Hosea 11. And Matthew 2:18 references another fulfilled prophecy from Jeremiah 31:15. And Matthew 2:23 reveals the fulfillment of Isaiah 11:1. 750 years before Jesus was born, God foretold through Hosea that He would come out of Egypt. Approximately 300 years before the birth of Christ, Jeremiah said there would be loud weeping coming from Ramah. And 720 years before Jesus was born through a virgin named Mary, God's Word predicted He would be a Nazarene. Only God in His sovereignty could put all these details into place through the incarnation of Jesus Christ. God has a unique way of accomplishing His will. He also has an amazing way of clarifying His purpose through His Word.

Jesus is the way, the truth, and the life. (John 14:6). He came into this world in a very specific way, and He is the only way to the Father. He is the truth because everything He says is true or comes true. Christ is the life because not only is He the giver of our next breath; He is also our reason for living. However, it is also interesting that Jesus came a specific way—born of a virgin. His birth fulfilled several prophecies of the New Testament because Jesus is the truth. Jesus' incarnation, crucifixion, and resurrection makes it possible for every sinner to be born again.

With all of this, one perplexing part surrounding Jesus' birth is Herod's killing of innocent children. Stanley Hauerwas states:

Perhaps no event in the gospel more determinatively challenges the sentimental depiction of Christmas than the death of these children. Jesus is born into a world in which children are killed, and continue to be killed, to protect the power of tyrants.[2]

We live in a fallen world full of death and darkness. The wages of our sins lead to death. Thus, death is a direct result of our flesh. But the Spirit brings life. Even in the birth of Jesus, we see the stark contrast between the evil in this world and the goodness of God.

God has a purpose for His people. He places His grace over our lives and then allows us the privilege of serving in His master plan. The greatest day of your life is the day you find His saving grace. The next greatest day is when you understand why He saved you and what He calls you to. God wants you to find your place in His grace!

There is a story surrounding the famed English architect, Sir Christopher Wren, when he was directing the building of St. Paul's Cathedral in London. Some of the workers were interviewed by a journalist who asked them, "What are you doing here?" The first said, "I'm cutting stone for three shillings a day." The second replied, "I'm putting ten hours a day in on this job." The third replied, "I'm helping Sir Christopher Wren build the greatest cathedral in Great Britain for the glory of God."[3]

It would benefit every believer to answer the same question regarding your purpose in life. "What are you doing here? Why did God pour out His grace all over your life? Why has He loved you into His Kingdom and blessed you with spiritual gifts and abilities? The answer to each question is—God has a plan for this life He has blessed you with. God created us all with a deep longing in our hearts that can only be fulfilled when we find our place in His plan. I pray that you find daily your place in His grace. When you do, you will know the joy that only a journey with Jesus can provide.

Questions:

1. Notice the following statement from Michael Grigoni's book, *Mary: Devoted to God's Plan*:

> Mary probably knew that she could no longer predict God's plan for her and her son. As she felt the first pangs of labor while tucked away in a stable, away from her home, family, and support, Mary understood that she would just have to be content with trusting Him.[4]

As you have looked at pictures of grace from the genealogy of Jesus, are you content in trusting Him? If not, how can you learn to trust Him more with the details of life?

2. Why is it that you can trust Him to forgive all your sins and give you eternal life in Heaven, but have a difficult time accepting His grace in place of your guilt and His blessings in the place of your burdens?

3. Spend some time in prayer today trusting His plan for your life while realizing you too are a picture of His grace!

Pictures of Grace

Notes

Day 1

[1] Sneed, J. (2017, June 23). *Quotes from Kyle Idleman's book "Grace is greater" – part 1.* jasonlsneed.com. https://jasonlsneed.com/2017/06/23/quotes-from-kyle-idlemans-book-grace-is-greater-part-1

[2] David T. Lamb, *Prostitutes and Polygamists: A Look at Love, Old Testament Style* (Grand Rapids, MI: Zondervan, 2015).

[3] Ibid.

Day 2

[1] Say, J. (2023, May 22). *Top 101 quotes about the grace of god (mercy).* Gracious Quotes. https://graciousquotes.com/grace-of-god/

Day 3

[1] Say, J. (2023, May 22). *Top 101 quotes about the grace of god (mercy).* Gracious Quotes. https://graciousquotes.com/grace-of-god/

[2] David T. Lamb, *Prostitutes and Polygamists: A Look at Love, Old Testament Style* (Grand Rapids, MI: Zondervan, 2015).

[3] Tom Fuerst, *Underdogs and Outsiders: A Bible Study on the Untold Stories of Advent* (Nashville: Abingdon Press, 2016).

[4] Tremper Longman III, *Genesis*, ed. Tremper Longman III, The Story of God Bible Commentary (Grand Rapids, MI: Zondervan, 2016), 471.

Day 4

[1] Yancey, P. (n.d.). *What's so amazing about grace? quotes by Philip Yancey.* Goodreads. https://www.goodreads.com/work/quotes/1616396-what-s-so-amazing-about-grace#

[2] Wilbur Glenn Williams, *Genesis: A Commentary for Bible Students* (Indianapolis, IN: Wesleyan Publishing House, 1999), 262–263.

[3] Tremper Longman III, *Genesis*, ed. Tremper Longman III, The Story of God Bible Commentary (Grand Rapids, MI: Zondervan, 2016), 472.

Day 5

[1] Sneed, J. (2017, June 23). *Quotes from Kyle Idleman's book "Grace is greater" – part 1*. jasonlsneed.com. https://jasonlsneed.com/2017/06/23/quotes-from-kyle-idlemans-book-grace-is-greater-part-1

Day 6

[1] Say, J. (2023, May 22). *Top 101 quotes about the grace of god (mercy)*. Gracious Quotes. https://graciousquotes.com/grace-of-god/

[2] R. Kent Hughes, *Genesis: Beginning and Blessing*, Preaching the Word (Wheaton, IL: Crossway Books, 2004), 454.

[3] Tremper Longman III, *Genesis*, ed. Tremper Longman III, The Story of God Bible Commentary (Grand Rapids, MI: Zondervan, 2016), 473.

Day 7

[1] Say, J. (2023, May 22). *Top 101 quotes about the grace of god (mercy)*. Gracious Quotes. https://graciousquotes.com/grace-of-god/

[2] Tremper Longman III, *Genesis*, ed. Tremper Longman III, The Story of God Bible Commentary (Grand Rapids, MI: Zondervan, 2016), 473.

[3] James Montgomery Boice, *Genesis: An Expositional Commentary* (Grand Rapids, MI: Baker Books, 1998), 897–898.

Day 8

[1] Wesley, J. (2016, October 28). *A wesleyan understanding of Grace*. ResourceUMC. https://www.resourceumc.org/en/content/a-wesleyan-understanding-of-grace#

[2] Bruce B. Barton, *Matthew*, Life Application Bible Commentary (Wheaton, IL: Tyndale House Publishers, 1996), 2.

[3] Warren W. Wiersbe, *Be Strong*, "Be" Commentary Series (Wheaton, IL: Victor Books, 1996), 34–35.

Day 9

[1] Lucado, M. (n.d.). *A quote from Grace for the moment.* Goodreads. https://www.goodreads.com/quotes/466244-when-he-says-we-re-forgiven-let-s-unload-the-guilt-when

[2] Joanna Harader and Michelle Burkholder, *Expecting Emmanuel: Eight Women Who Prepared the Way* (Harrisonburg, VA: Herald Press, 2022).

[3] David M. Howard Jr., *Joshua*, vol. 5, The New American Commentary (Nashville: Broadman & Holman Publishers, 1998), 97.

[4] Ibid, 98–99.

[5] Stephen J. Lennox, *Joshua: A Commentary in the Wesleyan Tradition*, ed. Alex Varughese, Roger Hahn, and George Lyons, New Beacon Bible Commentary (Kansas City: Beacon Hill Press, 2015), 80.

[6] Kenneth A. Mathews, *Joshua*, ed. Mark L. Strauss and John H. Walton, Teach the Text Commentary Series (Grand Rapids, MI: Baker Books: A Division of Baker Publishing Group, 2016), 22.

[7] Pekka M. A. Pitkänen, *Joshua*, ed. David W. Baker and Gordon J. Wenham, vol. 6, Apollos Old Testament Commentary (Nottingham, England; Downers Grove, IL: Apollos; InterVarsity Press, 2010), 126.

[8] Kenneth A. Mathews, 22–23.

Day 10

[1] Yancey, P. (n.d.). *What's so amazing about grace? quotes by Philip Yancey.* Goodreads. https://www.goodreads.com/work/quotes/1616396-what-s-so-amazing-about-grace#

[2] Warren W. Wiersbe, *Be Strong*, "Be" Commentary Series (Wheaton, IL: Victor Books, 1996), 38–39.

[3] Kenneth O. Gangel, *Joshua*, ed. Max Anders, Holman Old Testament Commentary (B&H Publishing Group, 2002), 31–32.

Day 11

[1] Say, J. (2023, May 22). *Top 101 quotes about the grace of god (mercy).* Gracious Quotes. https://graciousquotes.com/grace-of-god/

[2] Robert L. Hubbard Jr., *Joshua*, The NIV Application Commentary (Grand Rapids, MI: Zondervan, 2009), 126–127.

[3] David M. Howard Jr., *Joshua*, vol. 5, The New American Commentary (Nashville: Broadman & Holman Publishers, 1998), 115.

Day 12

[1] Kenneth O. Gangel, *Joshua*, ed. Max Anders, Holman Old Testament Commentary (B&H Publishing Group, 2002), 28.

[2] Richard S. Hess, *Joshua: An Introduction and Commentary*, vol. 6, Tyndale Old Testament Commentaries (Downers Grove, IL: InterVarsity Press, 1996), 106–107.

[3] Dale Ralph Davis, *Joshua: No Falling Words*, Focus on the Bible Commentary (Scotland: Christian Focus Publications, 2000), 27–28.

[4] Richard S. Hess, 106–107.

Day 13

[1] Say, J. (2023, May 22). *Top 101 quotes about the grace of god (mercy).* Gracious Quotes. https://graciousquotes.com/grace-of-god/

[2] James Montgomery Boice, *Joshua* (Grand Rapids, MI: Baker Books, 2005), 30.

Day 14

[1] Say, J. (2023, May 22). *Top 101 quotes about the grace of god (mercy).* Gracious Quotes. https://graciousquotes.com/grace-of-god/

[2] Sneed, J. (2017, June 23). *Quotes from Kyle Idleman's book "Grace is greater" – part 1.* jasonlsneed.com. https://jasonlsneed.com/2017/06/23/quotes-from-kyle-idlemans-book-grace-is-greater-part-1

[3] Gene A. Getz, *Fearless Leadership: Insights into the Life of Joshua*, Men of Purpose Series (Serendipity House, 2004), 29.

Day 15

[1] Alistair Begg and Elizabeth McQuoid, *Ruth*, Food for the Journey (London: IVP; Keswick Resources, 2017), viii–ix.

[2] Michael S. Moore, "Ruth," in *Joshua, Judges, Ruth*, ed. W. Ward Gasque, Robert L. Hubbard Jr., and Robert K. Johnston, Understanding the Bible Commentary Series (Grand Rapids, MI: Baker Books, 2012), 293.

[3] Alistair Begg and Elizabeth McQuoid, 11.

[4] Iain D. Campbell, *Ruth: A Devotional Commentary*, Exploring the Bible Commentary (Leominster: Day One Publications, 2010), 12.

[5] Stephen Davey, *Ruth*, ed. Lalanne Barber, Wisdom Commentary Series (Apex, NC: Charity House Publishers, 2013), 9.

[6] Iain D. Campbell, 14.

Day 16

[1] Stephen Davey, *Ruth*, ed. Lalanne Barber, Wisdom Commentary Series (Apex, NC: Charity House Publishers, 2013), 35.

[2] Alistair Begg and Elizabeth McQuoid, *Ruth*, Food for the Journey (London: IVP; Keswick Resources, 2017), 30–31.

[3] Stephen Davey, 34.

[4] Ibid, 35.

Day 17

[1] M. R. De Haan, *The Romance of Redemption: Studies in the Book of Ruth* (Grand Rapids, MI: Kregel Publications, 1996), 79–80.

[2] Iain D. Campbell, *Ruth: A Devotional Commentary*, Exploring the Bible Commentary (Leominster: Day One Publications, 2010), 75.

[3] Michael S. Moore, "Ruth," in *Joshua, Judges, Ruth*, ed. W. Ward Gasque, Robert L. Hubbard Jr., and Robert K. Johnston, Understanding the Bible Commentary Series (Grand Rapids, MI: Baker Books, 2012), 332.

Day 18

[1] Robert J. Morgan, *Nelson's Complete Book of Stories, Illustrations, and Quotes*, electronic ed. (Nashville: Thomas Nelson Publishers, 2000), 283.

[2] George Sweeting, *Who Said That? More than 2,500 Usable Quotes and Illustrations* (Chicago, IL: Moody Publishers, 1995).

[3] M. R. De Haan, *The Romance of Redemption: Studies in the Book of Ruth* (Grand Rapids, MI: Kregel Publications, 1996), 93–94.

[4] George Sweeting, *Who Said That? More than 2,500 Usable Quotes and Illustrations* (Chicago, IL: Moody Publishers, 1995).

Day 19

[1] Stephen Davey, *Ruth*, ed. Lalanne Barber, Wisdom Commentary Series (Apex, NC: Charity House Publishers, 2013), 10.

[2] Ibid.

[3] M. R. De Haan, *The Romance of Redemption: Studies in the Book of Ruth* (Grand Rapids, MI: Kregel Publications, 1996), 105.

[4] Ibid, 106.

[5] Iain D. Campbell, *Ruth: A Devotional Commentary*, Exploring the Bible Commentary (Leominster: Day One Publications, 2010), 119.

[6] Stephen Davey, 9.

Day 20

[1] Francis Frangipane, *The Shelter of the Most High* (Lake Mary, FL: Charisma House, 2008), 59.

[2] L. Daniel Hawk, *Ruth*, ed. David W. Baker and Gordon J. Wenham, vol. 7B, Apollos Old Testament Commentary (Nottingham, England; Downers Grove, IL: Apollos; InterVarsity Press, 2015), 27.

[3] Ibid, 23.

[4] Stephen Davey, *Ruth*, ed. Lalanne Barber, Wisdom Commentary Series (Apex, NC: Charity House Publishers, 2013), 97.

[5] Iain D. Campbell, *Ruth: A Devotional Commentary*, Exploring the Bible Commentary (Leominster: Day One Publications, 2010), 133–134.

Day 21

[1] Francis Frangipane, *Transformed in His Presence: 180 Daily Readings for Your Pursuit of God* (Lake Mary, FL: Charisma House, 2018).

[2] M. R. De Haan, *The Romance of Redemption: Studies in the Book of Ruth* (Grand Rapids, MI: Kregel Publications, 1996), 177–180.
[3] Ibid.

Day 22
[1] John G. Butler, *David: The King of Israel*, vol. Number Fifteen, Bible Biography Series (Clinton, IA: LBC Publications, 1998), 692.
[2] John Woodhouse, *2 Samuel: Your Kingdom Come*, ed. R. Kent Hughes, Preaching the Word (Wheaton, IL: Crossway, 2015), 285.
[3] Warren W. Wiersbe, *Be Restored*, "Be" Commentary Series (Colorado Springs, CO: Victor, 2002), 64–65.
[4] Tom Fuerst, *Underdogs and Outsiders: A Bible Study on the Untold Stories of Advent* (Nashville: Abingdon Press, 2016).
[5] Ibid.

Day 23
[1] Natalie Chambers Snapp, *The Bathsheba Battle: Finding Hope When Life Takes an Unexpected Turn* (Nashville: Abingdon Press, 2019).
[2] Charles R. Swindoll, *The Tale of the Tardy Oxcart and 1501 Other Stories* (Nashville, TN: Thomas Nelson, 2016), 522.

Day 24
[1] Charles R. Swindoll, *The Tale of the Tardy Oxcart and 1501 Other Stories* (Nashville, TN: Thomas Nelson, 2016), 523.
[2] Natalie Chambers Snapp, *The Bathsheba Battle: Finding Hope When Life Takes an Unexpected Turn* (Nashville: Abingdon Press, 2019).

Day 25
[1] Natalie Chambers Snapp, *The Bathsheba Battle: Finding Hope When Life Takes an Unexpected Turn* (Nashville: Abingdon Press, 2019).
[2] Ibid.
[3] Ibid.

Day 26

[1] Warren W. Wiersbe, *Be Restored*, "Be" Commentary Series (Colorado Springs, CO: Victor, 2002), 63.

[2] Charles R. Swindoll, *The Tale of the Tardy Oxcart and 1501 Other Stories* (Nashville, TN: Thomas Nelson, 2016), 523.

[3] Dale Ralph Davis, *2 Samuel: Out of Every Adversity*, Focus on the Bible Commentary (Great Britain: Christian Focus Publications, 2002), 155.

[4] Ibid, 151–152.

[5] Warren W. Wiersbe, 71.

[6] Dale Ralph Davis, 154.

[7] John Woodhouse, *2 Samuel: Your Kingdom Come*, ed. R. Kent Hughes, Preaching the Word (Wheaton, IL: Crossway, 2015), 327.

Day 27

[1] Natalie Chambers Snapp, *The Bathsheba Battle: Finding Hope When Life Takes an Unexpected Turn* (Nashville: Abingdon Press, 2019).

[2] John Woodhouse, *2 Samuel: Your Kingdom Come*, ed. R. Kent Hughes, Preaching the Word (Wheaton, IL: Crossway, 2015), 331.

[3] Ron Rhodes, *1001 Unforgettable Quotes about God, Faith, & the Bible* (Eugene, OR: Harvest House Publishers, 2011).

[4] J. D. Greear and Heath A. Thomas, *Exalting Jesus in 1 & 2 Samuel* (Nashville, TN: Holman Reference, 2016), 2 Sa 13–14.

[5] Dale Ralph Davis, *2 Samuel: Out of Every Adversity*, Focus on the Bible Commentary (Great Britain: Christian Focus Publications, 2002), 156–157.

[6] Ibid.

[7] John Woodhouse, 334.

Day 28

[1] Charles R. Swindoll, *The Tale of the Tardy Oxcart and 1501 Other Stories* (Nashville, TN: Thomas Nelson, 2016), 216.

[2] Ibid.

3 Leadership Ministries Worldwide, *2 Samuel*, The Preacher's Outline & Sermon Bible (Chattanooga, TN: Leadership Ministries Worldwide, 1996), 100.

Day 29

1 Stanley Hauerwas, *Matthew*, Brazos Theological Commentary on the Bible (Grand Rapids, MI: Brazos Press, 2006), 23.

2 David Platt, *Exalting Jesus in Matthew*, ed. Daniel L. Akin, David Platt, and Tony Merida, Christ-Centered Exposition Commentary (Nashville, TN: Holman Reference, 2013), Mt 1:1–17.

3 Tom Wright, *Matthew for Everyone, Part 1: Chapters 1-15* (London: Society for Promoting Christian Knowledge, 2004), 3.

4 Stanley Hauerwas, 26.

Day 30

1 Ben Witherington III, *Matthew*, ed. P. Keith Gammons and R. Alan Culpepper, Smyth & Helwys Bible Commentary (Macon, GA: Smyth & Helwys Publishing, Incorporated, 2006), 43.

2 Roger L. Hahn, *Matthew: A Commentary for Bible Students* (Indianapolis, IN: Wesleyan Publishing House, 2007), 54.

3 Myron S. Augsburger and Lloyd J. Ogilvie, *Matthew*, vol. 24, The Preacher's Commentary Series (Nashville, TN: Thomas Nelson Inc, 1982), 18.

Day 31

1 Ken Heer, *Luke: A Commentary for Bible Students* (Indianapolis, IN: Wesleyan Publishing House, 2007), 45.

2 Michael R. Grigoni et al., *Mary: Devoted to God's Plan* (Bellingham, WA: Lexham Press, 2012), Lk 2:1–20.

Day 32

1 Bruce B. Barton et al., *Luke*, Life Application Bible Commentary (Wheaton, IL: Tyndale House Publishers, 1997), 43.

2 Ibid, 47.

Day 34

[1] Bruce B. Barton, *Matthew*, Life Application Bible Commentary (Wheaton, IL: Tyndale House Publishers, 1996), 24.

[2] Edward Rowell, ed., *1001 Quotes, Illustrations, and Humorous Stories: For Preachers, Teachers and Writers* (Baker Publishing Group, 2008), 154.

[3] Bruce B. Barton, 20–21.

[4] Charles R. Swindoll, *The Tale of the Tardy Oxcart and 1501 Other Stories* (Nashville, TN: Thomas Nelson, 2016), 626–627.

Day 35

[1] Yancey, P. (n.d.). *What's so amazing about grace? quotes by Philip Yancey*. Goodreads. https://www.goodreads.com/work/quotes/1616396-what-s-so-amazing-about-grace#

[2] Stanley Hauerwas, *Matthew*, Brazos Theological Commentary on the Bible (Grand Rapids, MI: Brazos Press, 2006), 41.

[3] Robert J. Morgan, *Nelson's Complete Book of Stories, Illustrations, and Quotes*, electronic ed. (Nashville: Thomas Nelson Publishers, 2000), 800.

[4] Michael R. Grigoni et al., *Mary: Devoted to God's Plan* (Bellingham, WA: Lexham Press, 2012), Lk 2:1–20.

Made in the USA
Columbia, SC
07 November 2023

25609503R00091